Twayne's English Authors Series

Sylvia E. Bowman, *Editor*
INDIANA UNIVERSITY

Samuel Taylor Coleridge

(TEAS) 36

Samuel Taylor Coleridge

By VIRGINIA L. RADLEY

Russell Sage College

Twayne Publishers, Inc. :: New York

In Memoriam
Howard James Radley

Preface

One of the major problems confronting the student of the life and work of Samuel Taylor Coleridge is the sheer mass of material written not only by Coleridge, but also about him. For volume, perhaps no writer in the nineteenth century was writing more while at the same time finishing less. His failure to conclude, whether it be major poems, lecture series, or systematic expositions of his philosophy, critical theory, or theology is at one and the same time the curse and genius of the man.

Coleridge scholars seem to have fallen heir to the curse and, on occasion, to the genius of the master. In consequence, there have been brilliant studies of specific poems, but no overview of the poetry; there have been highly specialized studies of his philosophy, his politics, his criticism, but no overview of the prose. The current biography awaits completion as does, similarly, the Herculean task of editing the notebooks. The fact that so much remains to be done should come as no surprise to anyone remotely familiar with Coleridge's own works or with subsequent works about him, for the man was undoubtedly endowed with the most complex mind to be found among his contemporaries in the nineteenth century.

This present study is an attempt to set before the general reader an introduction to the life of Coleridge and to as much of his poetry and prose as can be covered within the practical limits of the studies in Twayne's English Authors Series. Such an avowed purpose limits the method primarily to description rather than to analysis and determines that the focus be for the most part upon Coleridge as writer rather than upon Coleridge as philosopher, political scientist, theologian, and the like. In general, the plan proceeds chronologically, taking up the early poems, the major poems, the drama, and then proceeding to the prose, with emphasis upon those works which pertain to his literary criticism and to his major philosophical tenets. An attempt has been made to show the development of his work and also to lead the more specialized student to those areas of scholarship appropriate to his interests.

To my colleagues in the English department, to the members of the Russell Sage College administrative and library staffs; to Miss Anne Edmonds and her staff at the library of Douglass College; to Dr. Hilde Siering for her assistance with Coleridge's "Germanics"; to Dr. Alek Hetko for his reading of my chapter on Coleridge's philosophy; to Miss Sydney Pierce for her unfailing patience in checking references for accuracy and for proofreading the manuscript; and to the many friends who have given both information and encouragement during the years this study was underway, my grateful appreciation.

Virginia L. Radley

Russell Sage College

Contents

Chronology

1772   Samuel Taylor Coleridge born October 21, in the vicarage at Ottery, St. Mary, Devonshire.

1775   Began formal education at Dame Key's Reading School.

1778   Attended Henry VIII Free Grammar School of which his father was head.

1782   July, admitted to Christ's Hospital School.

1791   October, entered Jesus College, Cambridge.

1793   Enlisted under pseudonym, Silas Tomkyn Comberback, in the King's Regiment, 15th Light Dragoons.

1794   Obtained a discharge from the King's regiment and returned to Cambridge. Left in December without a degree.

1795   January, moved to Bristol, married Sarah Fricker. January–November, lectured at Bristol on politics and history.

1796   Brought out *Poems on Various Subjects* as well as March–May issues of *The Watchman*.

1797   Annus Mirabilis: the wonderful year! Under influence of William and Dorothy Wordsworth. Composed "Ancient Mariner," formulating both "Christabel" and "Kubla Khan."

1798   September, Wordsworth and Coleridge bring out the *Lyrical Ballads* anonymously, while they are traveling through Germany with Dorothy Wordsworth and John Chester.

1799   February, Coleridge entered University of Gottingen, having by now separated from the Wordsworths; July, returned to England.

1800   Winter or spring, translation of Schiller's *Wallenstein*, finished late spring; another edition of *Lyrical Ballads* with Wordsworth's preface pre-fixed.

1803   Toured Scotland with Wordsworth.

1804   Left in May for Rome and Malta to return to England some two years later. Health impaired. Rheumatism and opium conspire against Coleridge.

1806 Returned to England; separates from wife.

1808 January–June, lectured at London Royal Institute on "Principles of Poetry," fragments remain.

1809 June, *The Friend* begun.

1810 *The Friend* ended.

1811 November, lecture series initiated on Shakespeare, Milton, and other poets.

1812 January, lecture series on English poets concluded; probably also lectured in this year on classic and romantic drama, a series of twenty-seven lectures now lost.

1813 *Remorse* (revision of earlier play, *Osorio*) performed at Drury Lane Theater.

1814 Beginning in 1813, probably lectured at Bristol on Shakespeare, Milton, and various political issues. Newspaper reports abound.

1815 State of health declining.

1816 April, took up residence with Gilmans at Highgate; June, brought out volume of poetry containing "Christabel," "Kubla Khan," "The Pains of Sleep."

1817 Published *Biographia Literaria,* "Sibylline Leaves."

1818 March, lectured on English poetry: Middle Ages to Restoration.

1819 December of 1818, began lectures on history of philosophy, ended March of this year.

1825 May–June, *Aids to Reflection.*

1828 Pamphlet on *Church and State.*

1834 July 25, died at Gillman residence, Highgate.

1840 *Confessions of an Enquiring Spirit* published.

CHAPTER 1

The Early Years to the Fall of Pantisocracy

IN 1772, when William Wordsworth was two years old, Blake fifteen, Kant forty-eight, Southey and Lamb not yet in this world, Samuel Taylor Coleridge was born on October twenty-first, at the vicarage of Ottery St. Mary, Devonshire. Youngest of ten children born of the second marriage of the Reverend John Coleridge, Samuel was always to exist as the baby brother, yet was always to resist the overpowering authority implicit in the fact of eight older brothers, one older sister, and three older half sisters.[1]

While still a baby of three, Coleridge was sent to Dame Key's reading school for an initial "at the mother's knee" education.[2] Three years later he transferred to the Henry the Eighth Free Grammar School, of which his father was head.[3] It was here that he began to read voraciously, a habit that was to continue and to increase in intensity throughout his life. At this time tales of adventure and romance appealed to the boy. Among other works, he is known to have read *Robinson Crusoe* and the *Arabian Nights' Entertainments*.[4]

In 1782, his father having died the year before, Coleridge left the Grammar School and matriculated at Christ's Hospital School. For some eight years this was to be his home; and from Charles Lamb's description, the school with its "blue and tasteless porritch," its meat "rotten-roasted or rare,"[5] was a place almost utterly devoid of warmth or cheer.[6] From memory, Lamb evokes a picture of the young Coleridge, "Logician, Metaphysician, Bard!" which indicates that even at that time Coleridge was no stranger to philosophy,[7] an interest which now took precedence over his earlier love of adventure. During Coleridge's stay at Christ's, he became almost inundated by the philosophical views of the third century Neo-Platonists whom he found for a time congenial to his tastes. At the same time, as might be expected, he noted a strong antipathy to Voltaire.[8]

Boyer, headmaster of Christ's, was known to be a strict disciplinarian, and penalties exacted for student misdemeanors often relied for emphasis upon the use of fetters and the whip.[9] Boyer's reputation was such that Lamb tells the story that when Boyer was on his deathbed, one of the masters made the remark, "Poor J.B.!—may all his faults be forgiven; and may he be wafted to bliss by little cherub boys, all head and wings, with no bottoms to reproach his sublunary infirmities." [10] Boyer's influence, however, had its meritorious side, and it is to this side that Coleridge is indebted. Indeed, it was at Christ's under Boyer, as Hanson tells it, that the ". . . profound logic of great poetry was dinned into his mind." [11] And Boyer was not the sole influence in this respect; it was here also that Coleridge became familiar with the sonnets of William Bowles, a revered clergyman of the day.[12]

Christ's Hospital School enjoyed the patronage of about seven hundred boys. Some two hundred and seventy-five of this number were sons of clergymen, as was Coleridge himself. His mother had wished him to enter the ministry, and for this reason he not only studied at Christ's but later matriculated at Jesus College, Cambridge, in 1792.[13] The schedule at Cambridge demanded and received Coleridge's serious attention; he acquitted himself well during the year in both a hard-working and productive way. For example, he studied mathematics for three hours each day and the classics from teatime until eleven at night, devoting this latter period to translating Anacreon, reading Pindar, and writing Greek verse. His efforts and talent received awards; namely, the Craven Scholarship of 1793 and the Browne Gold Medal for a Greek ode on the slave trade.[14] It was in 1793 also that "Lines on an Autumnal Evening" was composed.

Unfortunately, the successes of that first year at Cambridge were short-lived, for at some time during 1793 Coleridge left the university. A combination of debts and carousing, his early diligence having given way to these deleterious habits, no doubt prompted him to seek a dramatic oblivion.[15] Under a pseudonym, he enlisted in the 15th Light Dragoons, a life totally incompatible with his interests and talents and from which he had to be extricated by his brother's efforts.[16] Somewhat chastened, he returned to Cambridge by April 12 of the same year, and in June he visited Oxford, where he met the young Robert Southey;[17] thus began one of the major relationships of his life. The two young poets found an immediate kinship, as the following excerpt from a letter to Southey indicates: "I like not Oxford nor the inhabitants of it—I would say, thou art a Nightingale among Owls—but thou art so songless and heavy towards night, that I will rather liken thee to the Matin Lark—thy *Nest* is in a blighted Cornfield, where the sleepy Poppy nods it's [sic] red-cowled head, and the weak-eyed Mole plies his dark work—but thy soaring is even unto heaven." [18]

The alliance with Southey was to become a significant one in Coleridge's life, for Southey too was a radical young liberal. Both were much taken with the principles of *Liberté, Egalité, Fraternité* embodied in the revolutionary spirit of the time. Sympathetically disposed to the cause of freedom, these two young men conceived the idea of a utopian venture, Pantisocracy, and made plans to realize this ideal by projecting a community to be established on the banks of the Susquehanna River in America. Coleridge's letters during this period are replete with enthusiastic pronouncements in favor of this utopian ideal. Again he writes to Southey: "Well, my dear Southey! I am at last arrived at Jesus. My God! how tumultuous are the movements of my Heart—Since I quitted this room what and how important Events have been evolved! America! Southey! Miss Fricker!" [19]

Such letters show the bent of Coleridge's mind at this time. In his headlong rush into idealism, all parts must be fused into the whole. "America! Southey! Miss Fricker!"—the latter as necessary to this approximate Eden as Eve to Paradise. The plan was that Southey would marry Edith Fricker while Coleridge, conveniently, would marry her sister, Sarah. Not love alone, for "Even Love is the creature of strong motive," [20] but rather expediency; the end, Pantisocracy, would justify the means. Men inspired with a dream must have compatible female helpmates, and the liberal Fricker sisters were readily available.

As the idea of Pantisocracy gained momentum, Hucks, Allen, and Burnett, new acquaintances of the two young poets, also became its devotees.[21] Before long, however, Southey withdrew from the venture. He did so at the suggestion of William Wynn, ostensibly to study law, but actually because the scheme appeared to be more and more impracticable financially, and Wynn had promised him a legacy of one hundred and sixty pounds a year. With Southey's withdrawal and with the continuing lack of funds with which to support the venture, the plan was doomed to collapse.

The result of the scheme was that no utopian community was ever established on the banks of the Susquehanna. There were, however, some less tangible results. For example, Coleridge and Southey did collaborate on a play, *The Fall of Robespierre*,[22] and in spite of the collapse of Pantisocracy, Coleridge did marry Sarah Fricker, thereby laying up for himself a store of domestic unhappiness.[23] The fact of Southey's withdrawal distressed Coleridge and created an open breach between the two men. In a long, reproachful letter written in November, 1795, Coleridge explains the extent of his disappointment in Southey's action; using the eloquent past tense, "I did not only venerate you for your own Virtues, I prized you as the Sheet Anchor of mine!" [24]

Although Coleridge had met with disillusionment in the failure of Pantisocracy, had lost a friend, had left college, and had tied himself to a fundamentally incompatible wife, Pantisocracy did confirm in him his zest for liberalism and resulted in a series of publications and lectures devoted to liberal ideals. In March, 1796, Coleridge initiated a periodical, *The Watchman;* in May this liberal venture also folded for lack of funds.[25] Shortly before this period, Coleridge gave a series of lectures on politics and religion. The intent of these was to establish governments grounded in utopian ideals.[26] These lectures, unlike *The Watchman*, were comparatively well received; out of them grew the first prose publication, *Conciones ad Populum*.[27] These activities, in addition to the 1796 volume of poetry, *Poems on Various Subjects*,[28] all demonstrate Coleridge's initial political and literary ventures.

Thus ended the first period of Coleridge's literary life, a period not unlike that of any average young man of above average interest and talent in the areas of literature and politics.

I The Middle Years to Highgate

Failure, so constant a companion of Coleridge's later years, was just now beginning to make his acquaintance. February, 1796, began a tumultuous year of change and upheaval. What the Coleridges were to do for money became an incessant question. The letters of this time are full of frustration and frenzy. One excerpt from a letter to his friend, Josiah Wade, is illustrative of Coleridge's self-reproach and doubt: "I verily believe no poor fellow's idea-pot ever bubbled up so vehemently with fears, doubts and difficulties, as mine does at present. Heaven grant it may not boil over, and put out the fire! . . . The present hour I seem in a quickset hedge of embarrassments! For shame! I ought not to mistrust God! but indeed, to hope is far more difficult than to fear." [29] In still another letter in February, 1796, he wrote to Joseph Cottle, his publisher, of the need to "write for bread," of his wife's illness and her ensuing complaints.[30] In a letter to a friend, he wrote that the ". . . past life seems to me like a dream, a feverish dream!" [31] And in like manner, he cried out to Cottle, "The Future is cloud and thick darkness—Poverty perhaps, and the thin faces of them that want bread looking up to me!" [32] It was during this same period of storm and stress that he was composing the poem, "Religious Musings." Small wonder that his mind turned to religion and philosophy in these hectic times.

In keeping with this frenetic tenor of life, the Coleridges were moving around not only in thought, but also in actuality: from Clevedon to Bristol and in December, 1796, to Nether-Stowey. Financial vicissitudes became stabilized in this latter move by the acquisition of a pupil, Charles Lloyd, the spoiled and precocious son of the Birmingham Lloyds. Young Lloyd wished to become a poet-philosopher, and in exchange for tutelage his family was willing to remit to Coleridge eighty pounds per year. Coleridge planned to supplement this sum with forty pounds a year, which he hoped to glean from his publications.[33]

Fortunately, the house at Stowey had a garden which adjoined the fields of the gentleman farmer, Thomas Poole, who had been a friend of Coleridge from the early years and long would continue to be one. Many letters and much conversation were to pass between these two men; and it is Poole who served as the first Good Samaritan to the overly sensitive young poet.[34] Coleridge in December of 1796 wrote to Poole of his bodily miseries: "I am very poorly; not to say ill. My face monstrously swoln; my recondite Eye sits quaintly behind the fleshhill; and looks as little as a Tomtit's. And I have a sore throat that prevents me from eating ought but spoon meat without great pain—and I have a rheumatic complaint in the back part of my head and shoulders." [35]

Malaise, no stranger to Coleridge, and of a generalized nature, permeates the subject matter of the letters. Its specific characteristics are minutely described; violent nausea, diarrhea, dyspepsia, neuralgia, and constant other complaints began to intensify in this early year, 1796.[36] Campbell states that at this point Coleridge began to take laudanum, between sixty and seventy drops a day, to assuage the pain of neuralgia.[37] How many of Coleridge's troubles and how much of his consequent failure to accomplish the maximum can be ascribed to his general constitutional inadequacy has been the subject of much critical debate. This controversy apparently began when Thomas DeQuincey, a onetime intimate of the Coleridge–Wordsworth circle, stated that Coleridge took opium not for pain but rather for the pleasurable sensations its consumption brought about.[38] Lucy Gillman Watson, granddaughter of the physician who took care of Coleridge in his later years, quotes her grandfather saying, " 'Coleridge began the use of opium on account of bodily pain, acute rheumatism, and for the same reason continued it, till he had acquired a habit too difficult under his own management to control.' " She further points out that Gillman, in this instance, is a better authority than DeQuincey.[39] Elisabeth Schneider explores the extent to which Coleridge was influenced by opium when writing "Kubla Khan" and finds it inconsiderable.[40] The point of view held in this present study concurs with that of Watson and Schneider, that is, that no one under the deep and consistent influence of the drug could possibly have written either the quantity or the quality of work which Coleridge produced during this period. The next few years saw a great increase in both literary and social activities.

Coleridge at Stowey was a man of many roles: writer, farmer, preacher, nurse, and teacher.[41] But more important than these diverse activities was the friendship with those two Romantic luminaries, William and Dorothy Wordsworth. The Wordsworths had settled at Alfoxden and Coleridge had met them, thus beginning a memorable and productive relationship. The walks taken by the trio around Stowey are too well-known to demand extensive comment. Suffice it to say that here began the rich reciprocal relationship that was to culminate in a revolutionary poetry and poetic critique initiated by the two young poets and resulting in that renowned literary collaboration, *The Lyrical Ballads*. Before discussing this venture, however, it is well to note the composition of a significant single poem, "This Lime Tree Bower My Prison," one of the notable contributions of that year, 1797, known in Coleridge scholarship as the *annus mirabilis*. From this point forward, the life of Coleridge is for a time inextricably involved with that of the Wordsworths. Almost daily social intercourse with this remarkable brother and sister seemed to provide the catalyst to greatness, for it is during this period that Coleridge conceived his greatest poems, "Christabel," "The Rime of the Ancient Mariner," and "Kubla Khan," poems so distinctive and so different from his others that many generations of readers know Coleridge solely through them. "The Ancient Mariner," however, was the only one of the three to appear in *The Lyrical Ballads*.[42]

The publication of *The Lyrical Ballads* has become in retrospect such a significant event that it warrants comment. In 1798, a small book, published by Joseph Cottle, appeared; the price was one shilling and sixpence. No one but a small group of Cambridge colleagues knew that the poems were written by Coleridge and Wordsworth. Four of the twenty-three poems were Coleridge's; the rest, Wordsworth's.[43] At the time of publication, Coleridge and the Wordsworths were in Germany, oblivious to the public's reception of the volume, until Sarah Coleridge wrote, as Campbell tells us, "cheerily," " '. . . the *Lyrical Ballads* are not liked at all by any.' " [44] Nevertheless, the poems did find a small coterie of admirers; DeQuincey, Lamb, Hazlitt, Poole, Miss Hannah More, and Henry Crabb Robinson were among those who read the poems with enthusiasm, and the first edition was a total sellout. In general, however, most people found many of the poems in *The Lyrical Ballads* ridiculous, dull, or both, and it was not until 1836 that the reputation of the poets approximated what it has become today. In 1798, a writer such as Scott had more appeal for the public.[45]

In actuality, *The Lyrical Ballads* was born, as Emile Legouis explains, out of a need for money. In theory, however, the poems served as a protest against eighteenth-century rationalism and formalism. In retrospect, their publication stands as a landmark in literary history, for it clearly marks the onset of a new and revolutionary poetry. Like most innovations, the poems, although not appreciated at the time, were to achieve their proper measure of fame.[46]

The young poets themselves were undisturbed by the unenthusiastic reception of *The Lyrical Ballads*, for Coleridge was deeply engrossed in Germany, its culture and language, while Dorothy and William Wordsworth were busily comparing the German landscape with their beloved English countryside.[47] Coleridge's letters home indicate homesickness and a longing for the familiar.[48] In spite of this evidence, however, he was making the most of his opportunity to assimilate German culture and knowledge. He remained away from England for eleven months. During this time, his younger son, Berkeley, died in April, 1799, but still Coleridge did not return until July of that same year.[49] Upon his return, he managed to bolster the old friendship with Southey, staying with him and their respective wives for the better part of a month. Coleridge then moved to Greta Hall, Keswick, while the Wordsworths settled at now famous Dove Cottage. Part II of "Christabel" was completed in 1800 but not published until 1816. After this, Coleridge seemed to set aside poetry for a time.[50]

Thus began the second major phase of Coleridge's life. Once again he was in dire financial straits despite frequent loans from his friend, the admirable Thomas Poole; once again illness plagued him and he resorted to opiates;[51] once again, and now forever, domestic troubles assailed him. Indeed, he fell in love with Wordsworth's wife's sister, Sara Hutchinson. She became the great love of his life, but the situation was utterly hopeless. Divorce, then virtually unknown, was not to be thought of. Thus, rather than inspirational, the love was one of despair. "Dejection: an Ode," composed in 1802, was the poetic fruit of this doomed alliance.

Friendships with the Wordsworths, Poole, and Lamb continued. Letters to Godwin abounded.[52] Charles Lloyd was by this time out of the picture and now was only an annoyance to Coleridge. Particularly distressing to the poet in later years was Lloyd's fictional biography of Coleridge, entitled *Edmund Oliver*, which held the poet's frailties up to ridicule. There seemed to be other problems also. Although October in Keswick may be a blaze of color signifying health and abundance, in Coleridge's letters there are references to Wordsworth, to Lamb, and to himself as ill men.[53]

Campbell states in his biography of the poet that from 1802–3 Coleridge developed in intellectual power but that his imagination seemed distilled away.[54] This once-popular interpretation of Coleridge's waning poetic production has been tempered over the years. Nonetheless, Coleridge had enormous health problems during this time, if the letters can be believed. From 1801 on, the poet seemed to be reduced to a mass of boils, scrofula, edemic eruptions, rheumatism, and the like, his body violently and continually assailed by onslaughts of diarrhea.[55] Coleridge believed a trip to Malta might help assuage his physical anguish, and so he departed in April, 1804, visited Rome, and returned to England more than two years later. Although he had promised his friends much by way of publication, he had actually accomplished little over this period.[56] Indeed, to many of his friends, Coleridge appeared at this time to be in a state of decline. Promises to his publishers also amounted to little. He failed to write to his friends, and they became frantic from worry.[57] His relationship with his wife, never an ideal one, now became nonexistent, to the end that in 1808 he became separated from her, never to resume the relationship. Finally, in 1808 he began to work on a series of essays and articles later known in their published form as *The Friend*. On June 1, 1809, the first issue appeared, although six months behind schedule. Once again, the public was unimpressed and found the contents dull as they had earlier found those of *The Watchman* series to be. After issue twenty-seven, the series was discontinued.[58]

From 1810 until 1816, Coleridge moved in comparative obscurity. His livelihood, almost always dependent on friends, now became wholly so. His health, never robust, now became entrapped in a vicious war between actual illness and illness brought on by overindulgence in opium. In the winter of 1810, he availed himself of the hospitality of the Morgan family. Ostensibly joining them for a brief visit, he stayed with these good people intermittently for some six years. The letters of 1804–15 reflect a desperate and often maudlin self-pity. One to his benefactor, Morgan, tells of his inability to write, of his distress over the break with Wordsworth (which had earlier taken place), of his feelings of alienation from humanity;[59] another written in 1814 tells of his inability to find direction, of his prayers that he might soon be able to execute some piece of work.[60] On April 26, 1814, in a later letter to Cottle, Coleridge seems to break apart. His deep remorse, resulting from his failure to fulfill promises both literary and social, his candor in the matter of opium consumption, his wracked conscience, all bespeak the dark night of a tormented soul: "Oh God! how willingly would I place myself under Dr. Fox in his Establishment—for my Case is a species of madness, only that it is a derangement, an utter impotence of the *Volition,* and not of the intellectual faculties." [61] In 1814 another letter with tragic overtones best describes the poet's descent into a particular hell. Again to Morgan he wrote: "Such was the direful state of my mind, that (I tell it you with horror) the razors, penknife, and every possible instrument of Suicide it was found necessary to remove from my room!" [62] The rest of this letter blames opium for his state of mind, holding to the claim that the drug was not taken for pleasure but rather for relief from physical pain.

It remains a wonder that a man so afflicted produced anything at all. But Coleridge, despite these torments, did produce work worthy of consideration. To be sure, no major poems of high imagination were being conceived, but these are the years of the great Shakespearean criticism, of lectures in belles-lettres, fine arts, mythology, philosophy, and the years in which the drama, *Remorse*, and the magnificent *Biographia Literaria* were brought out.[63] These were also the years of Coleridge's *magnum opus*, tentatively called *Logosophia*, which, although it now exists in fragments only, then entailed great effort and serious attention.[64]

It is obvious that these recent works indicate a shift in the poet's interests. Whether this be owing to a deadening of talent, brought on by overindulgence in opium,[65] or to the fact that his mind had always been predominately philosophical rather than poetic, or to his alienation from those fonts of inspiration, the Wordsworths, or to his own lack of "volition," is a moot question.[66] The fact remains that few poems were being conceived during these years, and no major poem was forthcoming. Certainly, during these middle years, Coleridge's philosophical development began to broaden and deepen. As Lamb had indicated, Coleridge was interested in philosophy from Christ's Hospital School days onward. In those days, it was the Neo-Platonic school that absorbed his interests, apparently to such an extent that neither history nor poetry was permitted to supplant "metaphysics and psychology" as preoccupations.[67] To sort out the philosophical influences to which Coleridge succumbed is an onerous task and one largely beyond the scope of this study.

In brief, the first major influence was that of David Hartley's associationist psychology. Coleridge seems to have remained under this influence for at least two years. Baker, in his study, *The Sacred River*, marks these years as 1794–97.[68] Hartley's doctrine of associationism was constitutionally opposed to the essential Coleridge, and therefore in all probability he ultimately rejected it.

Lovejoy, however, makes the case for Hartley's continuing influence, even though other philosophical credos took precedence.[69] "Associationism," or the theory that mental happenings are initially happenings in the nervous system, was propounded by Hartley in his work, *Observations on Man,* published in two volumes, in London, 1749. These "happenings," or sensations, according to Hartley, are recorded on the organism and thus precipitate nerve disturbances or vibrations. From these vibrations, movement occurs and leaves minute traces or images etched on the brain. Simple ideas, generated by these sensations, combine infinitely to produce complex ideas which are more than the sum of the combination. According to this doctrine, poetic creativity is dependent upon the vast storehouse of memory. As a result, imagination is governed by association of ideas and images previously stored in the memory.[70] As shall be later seen, such a doctrine, with its materialistic foundation and overtones, would not long suffice for Coleridge, who was, after all, essentially a philosophical idealist.

From the influence of Hartley, Coleridge moved to that of Berkeley whose famous dictum, *esse est percipi,* also made its appeal to the young writer. To be is to be perceived means simply that nothing exists significantly except as it exists in the mind of a sentient being; hence data of the senses is insignificant until mind makes it significant. For example, the tree in the forest does not make a noise when it falls until the observer not only hears, but also *thinks* "noise" upon hearing it. Thus mind thinking "noise" creates noise.[71] In the *Biographia,* Coleridge states that he rejected both associationism and the philosophy of Berkeley as insufficient explanations of the ultimate nature of reality and of man's relationship to reality.[72]

Other philosophical influences to which Coleridge himself admits are those of Jacob Boehme, George Fox, and William Law. These men, he relates, ". . . contributed to keep alive the *heart* in the head; gave me an indistinct, yet stirring and working presentiment, that all the products of the mere reflective faculty partook of DEATH." [73] Such men, however, foreshadowed a kind of pantheism which Coleridge wished to avoid. He therefore skirted but never crossed the ". . . sandy deserts of unbelief." [74] Spinoza too, had attractions for Coleridge, but the influence was not a lasting one, for he could not accept Spinoza's doctrine of impersonal immortality. As Coleridge remarked, although his "head was with

Spinoza," his heart was with the more personal doctrines of St. Paul and St. John.[75] In addition, Fichte was not to be tolerated in view of his ". . . hyperstoic hostility to NATURE" [76] and his burning asceticism. Nor was Schelling to be wholly assimilated, although the best of that philosopher could be abstracted in all conscience and kept forever.[77] It was probably in 1800, while situated at Greta Hall, Keswick, that the greatest of all philosophical influences seized Coleridge in its giant grip. It was at that time that he began the study of Kant. One year later he began in earnest to study metaphysics, a study which was ultimately to conquer the poet of high imagination and produce that somewhat weighty "metaphysical Bustard" of the later years.[78]

There were of course other philosophical influences exerted on Coleridge, but those mentioned above crop up from time to time throughout his life and work and are therefore of first importance. A great amount of debate has occurred and continues to occur concerning Coleridge's indebtedness to philosophers: it should be stressed again and again, however, that Coleridge's "philosophy" is Coleridge's and none other's. Naturally, he was eclectic. Whatever was grist to his mill he took without apology and, regrettably, often without acknowledgment. What Coleridge did to Kant, for example, is no more in actuality than what Coleridge did to any philosopher or philosophy which appealed to him. That which he liked, he assimilated into his own thinking and henceforth made it his own. That which he did not like, he rejected or improved upon. Further exemplification and explication of this habit of mind must await the section on the philosophical writing.

Chaotic as the thought of the middle years was, and barren though these years were of great poetry, the later years in the life of Samuel Taylor Coleridge were in many respects least productive of all. They do not appear to be so because many of the works conceived of long before this period were then published.

II *The Later Years*

In 1816, Coleridge, ill in body and spirit, had the good fortune to be taken under the meticulous care of the physician, James Gillman of Highgate; he was to remain with the Gillmans until his death. Under the watchful and kindly supervision of Dr. Gillman, Coleridge began to get things done with dispatch. "Christabel," conceived in 1789; "Kubla Khan," also earlier conceived; and the

"Pains of Sleep" were all published in April of 1816. In 1817, the *Biographia Literaria,* written in approximately one year's time, was published; and in 1818, fourteen lectures on Shakespeare and poetics were given.[79] Despite this sign of renewed activity with its happy results, Coleridge again found himself in financial straits, unable to send money to his estranged wife and family.[80] The next few years were to emphasize those characteristics so baffling to his friends, his critics, his biographers. For the most part, Coleridge alternated between dreaming and talking. He dreamed of teaching philosophy to young men of great expectations; he dreamed of writing an epic poem on the siege and destruction of Jerusalem; in a sense, he dreamed of finishing "Christabel." [81] And he talked: with Gilman, with Wordsworth (the latter having visited him at Highgate), with Keats, in whose handclasp he sensed death.[82] All of this dreaming and talking amounted to little in comparison with the productivity of either the *annus mirabilis* or of the middle years. He did write for *Blackwoods,* and he did engage in fruitful discussions with his nephew, Henry Nelson Coleridge, which were to culminate in *Table Talk.*[83] In addition to this, he did work on *Confessions of an Inquiring Spirit,* probably during the year of 1824, but this material did not appear until 1840.[84] Another work, *Aids to Reflection,* came out in 1825. This latter was, according to Lucy Watson, not well received by the public; in fact, no reviewer took any notice of it at all. In America, however, the *Aids* was republished with an introduction by Dr. Marsh, then president of the University of Vermont, and was greeted with acclaim by those serious young theology students whose delight in the volume gave it its first popularity.[85]

From 1825 until his death, Coleridge stayed on at Highgate, enjoying a measure of prosperity and acclaim. An annuity from the Privy Purse plus the remuneration from publications of the *Aids* eased him financially. Along with this material comfort came religious solace. Coleridge moved more and more in the direction of orthodox Christianity, having now come full circle from atheism through Unitarianism to Trinitarianism. The pamphlet on the *Constitution of Church and State* not only indicated his interests at that time but also seemed to some to be the precursor of the Oxford Movement.[86]

The last four years of his life were spent, for the most part, confined to his bed in his room at Highgate. Friends visited often.

Letters were written continuously, one of them one half hour before he fell into a terminal coma.[87] The morning of July 25, 1834, at six o'clock, Samuel Taylor Coleridge left this world, leaving to posterity a vast number of poems, lecture notes, philosophical, religious, and political essays, some dramas, copious marginalia, notebooks, letters, and an unfinished *magnum opus* somewhat more mythical than substantial.[88]

CHAPTER 2

Coleridge in His Time: The Romantic
Tradition

ROMANTICISM is a multifaceted point of view[1] to which
Samuel Taylor Coleridge can be said for the most part to
have subscribed. Modern scholarship has of course done its best
either to cast out all reference to Romantic and Romanticism, or
to castigate thoroughly those elements which historically have
been said to constitute the point of view.[2] When all is said and
done, however, Romanticism is as good a term as any to describe
this very loosely structured point of view. In this study, Romanticism will be the label applied to that literary period roughly cir-
cumscribed by the years 1798–1832,[3] and Romantic will be the
term used for those English writers generally thought to incorporate in their writings many of the facets discussed below. In the
main, Blake, Coleridge, Wordsworth, Shelley, Keats, and with
grave qualification, Byron, can be labeled, for one reason or another, Romantic. It is the purpose of this present discussion to
look anew into the heart of the matter and to determine, by draw-
ing upon specific paraphrases from the Romantics' own writings,
corporate evidence of that which may be designated the Romantic point of view.

First of all, the Romantics postulated that the ultimate nature
of reality was spiritual. They were, therefore, philosophical idealists, and their mission, they felt, was to uncover this ultimate reality and make it known throughout their poetry and prose. The
ways of uncovering ultimate reality differed among them. One
way was to look to the microcosmic particular and thereby to
catch intimations of that totality, the macrocosmic general.
Wordsworth, for example, saw in the meanest flower that blows
thoughts that lay too deep for tears; indeed, in the whole of natural scenes of consummate beauty, he could feel a presence that
disturbed him with the joy of elevated thoughts. Keats saw in the
Elgin marbles a sun, a shadow of a magnitude, or he saw in the

Grecian urn evidence of that classical symmetry which bespoke the deeper message that beauty was truth, truth beauty. Shelley felt in the west wind a power capable of driving his dead thoughts over the universe, quickening them like ashes from an unextinguished hearth, scattering those now vital words among mankind; or he saw in the skylark a manifestation of the spirit of beauty, for bird, as such, it never was. Coleridge found in the magic of the lime-tree bower evidence of a thinly veiled Almighty Spirit; indeed in all of animated nature was possible evidence for him of organic harps whose intellectual breeze was at once the Soul of each and God of all. In such ways, all of these men saw in the particular a semblance of the general.

Another way of uncovering this inner reality (which for the Romantic constituted the really real) was to grasp the whole intuitively, to sense, for perhaps an instant only, the whole macrocosmic totality a priori. No celandines, daffodils, birds, or winds were necessary to this approach. Shelley's sudden grasp of intellectual beauty, which in that poem fell stunningly upon him, and his conviction that life like a dome of many-colored glass stained the white radiance of eternity, relied not upon his direct experience with natural objects, but rather upon his transcendent grasp of a profound spiritual truth.

It ought to be made clear, however, that the ultimate nature of reality was not only spiritual, but benevolently so. Therefore man too, like nature, had his spiritual dimension, for as nature was often emblematic of the reality beyond the seen, so man was not only emblematic of this reality, but also contained a part of this benevolent essence within him. Man was basically good and potentially perfectible. For this reason, the Romantics saw in certain men a manifestation of this innate goodness in proportion to the extent to which such men incorporated benevolent spirituality into their lives and actions. For most Romantics, those men who lived close to nature, and thereby to those unadulterated natural facts (themselves emblematic of spiritual facts), were more worthy to be chosen as subjects for poems than were those men who lived in the midst of teeming cities. Wordsworth was more apt than the other Romantics to utilize this approach. He therefore intentionally selected a shepherd, a highland girl, a leech-gatherer, and the like, and pointed up their essential goodness and purity, their plain living and high thinking. Coleridge put himself into the rural setting of the Lake District and of Clevedon; here he ruminated over his pensive Sarah in the idyllic garden at Clevedon and saw her as a maid whose simple faith seemed much more pure than that held by more sophisticated men.

Children too, not yet corrupted by the viscissitudes and adulterations of civilized life, were to the Romantics more glaringly good than were the mass of men. Examples of this are so well-known that there is little need to labor the point. Wordsworth's *Lucy Poems,* the little girl in "We Are Seven," the six-year's darling of a pigmy size, Coleridge's baby son, Hartley, in "Frost at Midnight," Blake's chimney sweeps and tiny babes in *Songs of Innocence,* all conspire to reiterate that children in their innocence reflect a spiritual origin and an innate goodness which bespeak continually that all beings come from God, who is their home. For the Romantics, then, a consideration of children in their innocence was another way of grasping that goodness which was an integral component of essential reality.

Nor were flowers, winds, simple folk, or children sufficient to convey this message. The fauna too played a part. Here sentimentalism, stemming from the Romantic attempt to point up the symbiotic relationship between man and creatures, often intruded into Romantic verse. For example, Blake's Robin Red Breast in a cage put all of heaven in a rage; Coleridge's young donkey was somewhat more significant than a mere beast of burden, and the albatross and the water snakes were more significant than what they appeared to be. In point of fact, though this may seem a *reductio ad absurdum,* the English Romantics would have had no trouble understanding the American Emerson's statement that there was an occult relationship between man and the vegetable. There was equally for the Romantics an occult relationship between man and nature, man and man, man and beast, and any combination thereof. This relationship was a spirit of oneness and beauty manifest in the Many yet emanating from the One.

Now obviously, this way of looking at man and nature makes certain demands on the individual. These demands could be met only through invoking that power to both perceive and create which the Romantics called *Imagination.* Professor Bowra finds this belief in the power of imagination to be that which distinguishes English Romantics from their eighteenth-century literary predecessors.[4] Professor Tuveson, in his recent study, *The Imagi-*

nation as a Means of Grace, corroborates Bowra's contention by adding that the English Romantics devoted their efforts to those particulars which were capable of yielding up universal truths, whereas the eighteenth-century neo-classical writers concentrated on conveying general truths by considering the universal in man and nature.[5] The power that permitted English Romantics to see the universal in the particular was that of imagination. Samuel Johnson might well be interested in letting observation with extensive view survey mankind from China to Peru, but Samuel T. Coleridge could learn as much about the vanity of human wishes or of human nature per se by considering a single leaf in a lime-tree bower. In effect, the power that enabled him to see the general in the particular was that which lay within the domain of the creative process and which he too called imagination. And for the English Romantics, this was a *creating* as well as a perceiving power. To them the mind and being were active in the creation of the work of art, the poem, not passive as the eighteenth-century philosopher Locke believed. To the Romantics, mind was no *tabula rasa* upon which mere sensory impressions were recorded. No such concept would suffice for them in explanation of either man's highest creation, poetry, or his highest function, the ability to grasp truth.

The Romantic point of view, then, encompassed the conviction that ultimate reality was spiritual and was reflected not only in the beauties and order manifest in nature but also in the deeds and being of good men. That power which enabled men to grasp either in part through contemplation of these things and modes, or *in toto* through intuitive perception, was termed imagination. This power is the same which enabled the poet to reshape the forms of nature and actions of men and add the gleam to produce that beauty incarnate in a work of art.

The Romantic point of view was indeed multifaceted, and some of its facets were less glittering, less significant, than those discussed above. The wish to rise above the common-sense world of the understanding was implicit not only in the postulate that the ultimate reality was spiritual but also in the conviction that the imagination was both perceptive of what is and recreative on its own. The wish to transcend the world of the understanding, of the commonplace, might be realized by contemplating natural beauty, the lives of simple men, the innocence of children, and the symbiotic relationship between man and animals. Another facet, also reliant upon imagination for its being, was that wish to rise above the commonplace and common sense by resorting to the extraordinary, that is, to the un-common sense. When the Romantics took this direction, they created a world decidedly remote from the known world. They turned away, as it were, from the natural supernatural to the supernatural supernatural.[6] This second world, also a world dependent on the creative power of imagination, might be remote in time and place, or alien, or bizarre, or grotesque—or any combination of those elements which heighten the contrast between the two worlds. Wordsworth's "Laodamia" involved classical figures, one lodged in the real world of the past and one lodged in the underworld of the past. Keat's "Eve of St. Agnes," set in the Middle Ages, is remote in both time and in its medieval romantic elements, as is his poem, "La Belle Dame Sans Merci," which has the added bizarre element of the "demon lover." His "Lamia" utilized the witch-snake motif and a classical setting. Shelley's "Sensitive Plant" imbued a garden with personal qualities and the plants with human sentience. Byron's "Manfred" starred an extraordinary man of supernatural power. Many are the examples, too numerous for extended comment. Coleridge's "Kubla Khan," "Lewti," "Christabel"; Blake's "Book of Thel," and the like, all belong in varying degrees to the world of the remote, the strange, the bizarre, and thus emphasize the supernatural supernatural. In this fashion an interest in the uncommon sense was also a part of the Romantic point of view.[7]

For obvious reasons, members of the eighteenth-century–neoclassical literati would have looked askance at such extreme emphasis upon the exceptional and particular.[8] Eighteenth-century writers were interested primarily in universals, in looking at nature as the mirror of universal truth seen not in its particulars, that is, in celandines, daisies, birds, one man's life, or remote regions of the past, but rather in the ordered harmony of sun, moon, stars, and seasons, and in the lives of men in general. For the eighteenth-century man of letters, the mission was to view the world with an ample supply of reason and common sense always at the fore. Man might imitate nature, which was the best way; or he might imitate those ancients who had imitated nature. But man should not attempt to create out of nothing, for such whimsy was not to be trusted. It was the general, the seen, which should be of interest to man, not the particular or the unseen, which was often "imagined." The balance and order seen in nature was what counted and what constituted both reality and beauty. Extremes of any kind were to be most assiduously avoided. Man was not unlimited in the eyes of the eighteenth-century–neo-classicists. He was placed on an isthmus of a middle state, suspended in the vast Chain of Being between angels and beasts. Only by dint of reason and common sense could man achieve that balance requisite to his station in life and to his place in the natural order. Extremes and excesses, whether of passion or imagination, would serve only to make man's status more difficult to maintain.

Coleridge stands between this eighteenth-century point of view on the one hand and the extreme Romantic point of view on the other. Not only is this true, but in addition he is not the extremist *within* his own period that Shelley became later on or that Wordsworth appeared to be in certain of his early poems. It would be unfair to say that Shelley swept into abstraction almost instantaneously, whereas Wordsworth dawdled almost interminably over particulars before moving on; but to make this statement is to indicate the directions of their extremes within the period. Coleridge in a sense sought to reconcile the extremist view represented by the early Wordsworth and that opposite extreme represented by the later Shelley. This point can be seen in Coleridge's conception of the function of the poet. For Coleridge, the poet asks that the reader, in reading a poem "professedly ideal," look for the "balance of the generic with the individual," or, to use his term, to effect a "reconciliation of opposites." [9] The generic, when applied to a created character, makes this being ". . . representative and symbolical, therefore instructive . . . it is applicable to whole classes of men." The particular, on the other hand, gives to this character ". . . living interest; for nothing *lives* or is *real*, but as definite and individual." [10] Coleridge here agrees with the mentor of the eighteenth-century men of letters, Aristotle, but he adds to that classicist's emphasis on the ideal an equal emphasis on the particular.

Such contentions may well provide the key to Coleridge's twentieth-century reputation. Certainly, they demonstrate that he strove for balance and in so doing attempted to avoid not only the extreme confines of neo-classical genres, but also the extreme excesses of ultra-Romantic particulars. The attempt to pull together the general and the particular, reconcile them into a higher third, and thus produce great works of art, is one which marks Coleridge as the unique poet of the poems of high imagination. With Coleridge, as later with Keats, this attempt was not always successfully realized and in fact was almost totally unrealized before the poems of the *annus mirabilis.* For this reason it is interesting to look at his juvenilia and minor poems in an effort to see these developmental aspects of his early work and to watch his progression to artistic realization in the poems of high imagination.

CHAPTER 3

Juvenilia and the Minor Poems

THE poems of Samuel Taylor Coleridge written before the publication of the *Lyrical Ballads* are, for the most part, notable only for diversification of subject and for the evidence in them of strongly traditional influences. There are two groups which form exceptions to this minor poem potpourri. Group I is made up of "The Eolian Harp" (1795, 1796), "Reflections On Having Left a Place of Retirement" (1796), "This Lime-Tree Bower My Prison" (1797, 1800), and three poems published in April, 1798: "France: An Ode," "Fears In Solitude," and "Frost At Midnight." [1] The following chapter will consider these poems under the heading, "Major Minor Poems."

Other poems belonging to the pre-*Lyrical Ballad* period which, though less significant than those above, are also deserving of treatment are: "Lines On An Autumnal Evening" (1796), "Sonnets On Eminent Characters," "Monody on the Death of Chatterton" (first version written, 1790; last version published, 1796), "The Destiny of Nations" (1796, 1817), "Ode to the Departing Year" (1796), and "Religious Musings" (1794, 1796). These poems, which form Group II, or the "Lines . . ." group, are not as appealing belletristically as are those in Group I, the "Eolian Harp" group, but they are nonetheless historically interesting for the light they throw on Coleridge's philosophical development.

I *Juvenilia*

Those poems which fall outside these two groups constitute the potpourri proper and deserve notice only as curiosities. Within this category are poems on a variety of subjects, namely: noses, perspiration evoked as a result of a ride in a stage coach, a mathematical problem, a young ass, a tea-kettle, a lady weeping, pain, disappointment, a nurse in the school infirmary, various imitations of poets of yesteryear, flowers, and life. [2] These poems are memorable only for their diversity of subject and treatment. They are illustrative of the chaotic experimentation of the young Coleridge not yet a poet but hopeful of becoming one.

II *Minor Poems*

For Coleridge, the act of becoming a poet was consistent in over-all progression, although sporadically so in appearance. That there was development cannot be denied. That the Juvenilia and many of these early poems were Janus poems is also true; they look backward in recapitulation of past convention and forward in anticipation of those innovations which Coleridge would later make. The poems in the "Lines" group stand in illustration of the Janus characteristic. In the first draft of "Lines" (entitled initially "An Effusion At Evening"), Coleridge uses the term *Imagination*.[3] In the final version, he changes this to *Fancy*.[4] At this point, he may have begun to evolve his famous distinction between the two terms, although there is no way of proving this. He appears, however, to use these terms interchangeably in these early versions, much in the same way the terms were switched around at random in the mid-eighteenth century. Other retrospective elements in the poem are: a heavy reliance upon personification illustrated by the antithetical qualities of "Disappointment" and "Joyance"; an overuse of traditional nature imagery more characteristic of the seventeenth century; a series of heavily contrived couplets; and, finally, a generous sprinkling of archaic verbs.

The gist of the poem, which is not always clear, unfolds when Fancy is admonished by the poet to quit the "purple clouds," to check her "vagrant wing," to "aid [the] Poet's dream." In short, Fancy is admonished to act the sorceress and thereby to imbue the landscape with beauty in order that the "Spirits of Love" so essential to poetic creation will descend and inspire the poet. To what end is never fully developed. It is clear, however, that nature undergoes a sentimentalizing process and is the less for it, as the following lines affirm:

> Dear native brook! like Peace, so placidly
> Smoothing through fertile fields thy current meek!
> Dear native brook! where first young Poesy
> Stared wildly-eager in her noontide dream!
> Where blameless pleasures dimple Quiet's cheek,

As water-lilies ripple thy slow stream!
Dear native haunts! . . . [etc.]   (ll. 81–87)

What is clear here is that this poetry, as poetry, is certainly inferior to that which distinguishes the poetry of the "Major Minor Poems," though in many respects it is on a par with that comprising the Juvenilia. Such overworked clichés: "loose luxuriance of her hair," "the wondrous Alchemy of Heaven," "that passion-warbled song," and a host of others combine with the other characteristics cited to make the poem reminiscent of another age, yet meretriciously so.

Although "Lines . . ." is a Janus poem by implication, it is chiefly retrospective rather than prospective. There is little in it that anticipates the Romantic mode of the great period other than the interjection of the personal element illustrated by the following lines:

Scenes of my Hope! The aching eye ye leave
Like yon bright hues that paint the clouds of eve!
Tearful and saddening with the sadden'd blaze
Mine eye the gleam pursues with wistful gaze:
Sees shades on shades with deeper tint impend,
Till chill and damp the moonless night descend.
(ll. 101–106)

Something might, of course, be made of *gleam,* a favorite word of the Romantics, and therefore prospective. There is here, however, no conscious use of gleam in this sense, although it appears in the poem three times. The use here has none of the significance ascribed to the word by Wordsworth in *Elegiac Stanzas,* in speaking of the ". . . gleam,/ The light that never was, on sea or land." [5] Indeed, the reader receives in the Coleridge poem no impression of the poet's having an acute awareness of nature. There is little in the poem that is distinctly autumnal, little that bespeaks the Romantic eye creating and recreating in its appraisal of an actual scene. The poem stands as a kind of exercise in imitation. Retrospective in imagery, rhyme scheme, and tone, the poem might be said to be prospective in its concern with the efficacious power of love, a theme which will continue to permeate the poetry and philosophy of Coleridge in the years to come. The intimations seen in the poem, "Lines . . . ," of this power of love, provide the key, if there is any key, to an understanding of Coleridge in his several roles: Man, Poet, Religioso, Philosopher. The development of this theme, however, must await the "Major Minor Poems"; and, for its full maturation, the poems of high imagination.

"Sonnets on Eminent Characters," taken as a whole, are also interesting historically for what they illumine of Coleridge's early interests.[6] For this reason, these are included in the "Lines . . ." group. These sonnets are addressed to those whom Coleridge admired: Erskine, Burke, Priestley, La Fayette, Koskiusko, Pitt, Bowles, Mrs. Siddons, Godwin, Southey, Sheridan, and Stanhope. As might be expected in view of Coleridge's youthful interests in liberal movements, the first six sonnets concern themselves with the state and status of freedom, favoring its protagonists and castigating its antagonists. The sonnet to Bowles (both versions) thanks him for his sweet influence on the young poet, for awakening in his heart the qualities of sympathy and love for his fellow men, which in later days are to sustain and soothe him. The final couplet, "Like that great Spirit, who with plastic sweep/ Mov'd on the darkness of the formless Deep!"[7] contains the germ of that belief which was to become identified with Coleridge, in a word, his "metaphysic." A fuller discussion of this occurs in Chapter IX; but cursorily defined, it is Coleridge's belief that there is form which gives form to the formless; there is spirit which gives meaning to the meaningless; there is reality behind appearances; and that only the combination of heart with head, impelled by imagination, can produce a great poem, a great work, a great life. Here lies partial confirmation of Coleridge's involvement with one of the more significant tenets of Romanticism.

The sonnet to Southey lauds that young man for those melodies of his which serve Coleridge as do beauteous natural scenes, that is, melodies evocative of pleasurable sensations which recur continually through recollection of the poems. The power of poetry to evoke not only initial pleasure but also those memories concomitant with other pleasures was, of course, a popular conception of the Romantics as a whole. Undoubtedly, for Coleridge, Hartley's associationist psychology is also commensurate with the idea expressed in the following excerpt from the sonnet to Southey:

> . . . But O! more thrill'd, I prize
> Thy sadder strains, that bid in MEMORY'S Dream
> The faded forms of past Delight arise;
> Then soft, on Love's pale cheek, the tearful gleam
>
> Of Pleasure smiles—as faint yet beauteous lies
> The imag'd Rainbow on a willowy stream.   (I, 87, ll. 9–14)

Historically interesting also are the two versions entitled "Monody on the Death of Chatterton." The first version, written at Christ's Hospital when Coleridge was approximately sixteen years old, is puerile in tone, peppered with exclamation marks, and fraught with those personified qualities so devastating to esthetic appeal: Humour, Pity, Neglect, Want, Fancy, Oppression, and the like. The poem is a typical schoolboy diatribe against the injustices, real or imagined, met by a young prophet (here Chatterton) in his native land.[8] In the first version, young Coleridge beseeches the spirit of the youthful Chatterton as follows:

> Grant me, like thee, the lyre to sound,
> Like thee, with fire divine to glow—
> But ah! when rage the Waves of Woe,
> Grant me with firmer breast t'oppose their hate,
> And soar beyond the storms with upright eye elate!
>   (I, 15, ll. 86–90)

It would be difficult to conceive of the young Milton writing so, although not at all difficult to conceive of the young Shelley producing such. And yet even as the shrieking lines bespeak the onset of a brand of poetry not unknown to young Romantics, still youth in any age is almost universally declamatory, emotional, sensational, idealistic. In view of this, the poem can be said to be both anticipatory of nineteenth-century frenetic Romanticism and reflective of the eighteenth-century emphasis upon universal characteristics.

The second version of the "Monody . . ." is much more restrained (although not necessarily more poetic); many of the personified qualities have been pruned away.[9] The tone is far less shrieking, though far more wallowing. As poetry, this second version, although more temperate, is not significantly better; moreover, this version has not the excuse of having issued from the pen of a very young poet. The poem is some fifty-one lines longer, yet there is still no unity except that of subject. Even this is somewhat in doubt, as the intrusion of the Susquehannah River in the last few lines would indicate. In this version, Coleridge, having lamented the death of the young Chatterton (as in the first version), having hoped himself to be stronger than the "marvelous boy," projects and sees himself already established on the banks of the Susquehannah raising a "Cenotaph" in memory of Chatterton and musing ". . . on the sore ills [he himself] had left behind" (I, 131, ll. 158–165). Indeed both "monodies" on Chatterton reflect small promise of the "Major Minor Poems" and no promise at all of the great poems to come. They are interesting in that they show some awareness of the predicament of the artist in society, of man's inhumanity to man, and of a need peculiar to Coleridge to be stronger than those who have fought and failed in the good fight.

In this same category also lie the two religious-political poems, "The Destiny of Nations" [10] and "Ode to the Departing Year." [11] Some two hundred and five lines of the former constituted a part of Book II, "Joan of Arc," a dramatic poem composed in collaboration with Southey. The remaining two hundred and twelve lines formed a part of an unpublished poem, "The Vision of the Maid of Orleans." The whole of the poem was first published in 1817. Like so many of Coleridge's poems this too is unfinished; it ends in a collection of fragments intended to have rounded out the work. The main subject is the maid of Orleans; the main theme, her courage and victory over other humans and over her own mean circumstances. She is different, as the following lines aver: "From her infant days,/ With Wisdom, mother of retired thoughts,/ Her soul had dwelt" (I, 137, ll. 139-141). A young girl in Nature, she has learned more than "Schools could teach" of man, his vices and virtues, his dignity, and those indignities flesh is heir to (ll. 153–155). Though Joan is good, the World is far less so. She is the lone pilgrim who here questions the human condition and strives to improve it (ll. 179–271). She is extraordinarily sensitive. Perhaps for this reason, perhaps because it was so recorded, a "mighty hand" is "strong upon her," and she is among the elect of God, destined to lead men to greater things (ll. 261–277). Such is the gist of the poem as it rambles on. Such lines seek oblivion except for their historical significance. As poetry, they contain faults similar to those manifest in the Chatterton monodies: an abundance of personification, forced diction, contrived rhymes, sentimentality, and lack of unity. Within the greater context of the Romantic point of view, however, Coleridge's "Maid" is important. Isolation, loneliness, a feeling of alienation—all characterize the Harolds, Manfreds, Lucys, Michaels, and Mariners of a later-day Romanticism. Joan therefore belongs to the main stream of Romanticism, if only as anticipatory of the deluge to come. Both retrospective and prospective are the following Janus-lines which address God in stentorian phrases. He is called: "Auspicious Reverence," "Great Father," "only Rightful King," "King Omnipotent"—all retrospective labels. More typically Coleridgean and also more closely Romantic are the less personalized terms: "the One," "the Good," "the Will Absolute" (ll. 1–6). The poet refers to these appelations as a symphony which requires the soul, its best instrument, to play; thus from the dome of freedom the harp is seized, ". . . With that/ Strong music, that soliciting spell" (ll. 10–11). Significant in Coleridge's later world view, and pointing toward that view, are the lines concerning freedom, its source and its role. Freedom comes from God, though granted to man to achieve through choice. Another important element in the poem is Coleridge's concept of the function of man's physical senses. To him the world is one vast alphabet which man's infant mind must learn to read, for its symbols are the appearances behind which glows the true reality:

> For all that meets the bodily sense I deem
> Symbolical, one mighty alphabet
> For infant minds; and we in this low world
> Placed with our backs to bright Reality,
> That we may learn with young unwounded ken
> The substance from its shadow.   (ll. 18–23)

The philosophical substructure of "The Destiny of Nations" is quite openly a conglomeration of St. Paul, Plato, Plotinus, and by this time, undoubtedly, Berkeley. The poem is therefore historically significant in a study of Coleridge's development, for it demonstrates the initial or embryonic stage of that ideology which some critics call the Coleridge demon and which others affirm the Coleridge saint. Whichever way one chooses to look at this aspect of the Coleridge "metaphysic," there can be no doubt but that it is an aspect which demands serious attention.

"Ode to a Departing Year" in its opening lines also incorporates the idea that the unseen is a real and crucial force. In these lines the poet prays to the Divine Providence who orders events in time: "Spirit who sweepest the wild Harp of Time!/ It is most hard, with an untroubled ear/ Thy dark inwoven harmonies to hear!" (ll. 1–3, p. 160). In this poem, as in "The Destiny of Nations," the poet solicits the services of the harp, an instrument, like the lute, peculiarly adaptable to his message. The subject of the "Ode" is a familiar one, that is, the wretchedness of sick, sorrowing humanity, and what those who suffer can do to ameliorate that condition. The poet calls upon mankind to devote its thoughts and sympathies not to individual private sorrows but, rather, to those general ills and afflictions which are the lot of the whole.[12] Section III of the poem contains a diatribe against the Empress of Russia, referred to as "insatiate Hag," and shows Coleridge to be here in sympathy with France as the Empress was not. The poem then enumerates the many evils extant at the time and prophesies that England too will eventually fall prey to avarice and moral cowardice (ll. 135–49). In the concluding lines, the poet flies from that in which he has had no part, the corruption and dissolution, and "recentre[s]" his soul "In the deep Sabbath of meek self-content" (ll. 158–59).

"Religious Musings," written on Christmas Eve, 1794, also belongs to the "Lines . . ." group, for it too would have difficulty standing on its own poetic merits.[13] The poem, while again illustrative of the thoughts current with Coleridge at the time, contains some of the common blights which characterize the poems belonging to this group. Again, the abundance of personification, the traditional allusions, and the vast number of lifeless metaphors almost inundate the reader in a sea of turgidity. In the opening lines, Christ's nativity provides the stimulus for the poet's musings, an appropriate stimulus on Christmas Eve. After this departure, there occurs a melee in which the influences working on Coleridge, his vast and capricious reading, his devotion to diametrically opposed philosophies, become both apparent and confusing.

Initially, Christ is lauded, with Miltonic overtones, as the suffering, though heroic, savior of mankind. In His face, as in to a lesser extent all nature, shines the true impress of God the Father. All external nature and matter become symbols of the "Great Invisible" (ll. 9–27). This "Great Invisible" will become visible only when man learns to read the symbols correctly, and he can do this only through the requisite help of Christ's love. The efficacy of this latter will illumine shadows by the light of faith and love in order to annihilate self. In this way self becomes supplanted by God. "We and our Father one" (ll. 29–44). The concept of the one behind the many, indivisible yet divisible, seen only in fragmentary form when seen at all, was taken either directly from Plato or, more probably, from Plotinus and the Cambridge Platonists. "Religious Musings" is shot through with many examples of variations on the same theme as the following excerpts demonstrate: "There is one Mind, one omnipresent Mind,/Omnific, His most holy name is Love" (ll. 105–6). The next example reads, " 'Tis the sublime of man,/ Our noontide Majesty, to know ourselves/ Parts and proportions of the one wondrous whole!" (ll. 126–28). Another in support of the same motif reads:

> Believe thou, O my soul,
> Life is a vision shadowy of Truth;
> And vice, and anguish, and the wormy grave,
> Shapes of a dream! The veiling clouds retire,
> And lo! the Throne of the redeeming God
> Forth flashing unimaginable day
> Wraps in one blaze earth, heaven, and deepest hell.
>   (ll. 395–401)

This theme too is central to the Coleridge "metaphysic," but it remained by no means unique with him. Other Romantics resorted to it with gusto. For example Shelley in the "Hymn to Intellectual Beauty," Wordsworth in the "Immortality Ode," are two notable subscribers. The idea took hold on Coleridge's mind long before his ventures into German idealism. What was to become an integral part of Coleridge's philosophy can be seen here in "Religious Musings" in its seminal form. In addition to incorporating this central idea, the poem extols the virtues of those who have faith and meek piety and are therefore "of the spiritually elect." Among those so identified by Coleridge in the poem are Milton, representing the poet of steadfastness, and three men of science who, in his opinion, rose above the mundane: Newton, Hartley, and Priestley. Again the emphasis is upon responsible men, men who are responsible to self, man, and God.

Presumably, Coleridge early felt the dilemma posed by conflicting beliefs, namely: man's responsibility to achieve self-discipline and to contribute significantly to the welfare of his fellowmen versus man's desire for individual freedom and for the creative expression which occurs when individual freedom is granted full sway. These poems in the "Lines . . ." group chiefly emphasize the former, that is, responsible citizenship. Chatterton, for example, was weak, creative, yet self-destructive. The sonnets in the "Lines . . ." group emphasize, on the other hand, the responsible man while condemning the tyrant. Joan, the maid, is strong and responsible. England, though still somewhat responsible, is gravely in danger of becoming less so, as Russia has become less so through the tyranny of the Empress. In "Religious Musings," the poet feels a responsibility to discipline his creativity, thereby to produce verse worthy of his final entry into heaven's "mystic choir." All of the poems in the "Lines . . ." group are unsatisfactory (though in varying degrees) to the reader. They are not appealing esthetically. They are, however, of interest to the literary historian and to the student of Coleridge. Certainly, they are not illustrative of Coleridge's mature poetry, but they do serve to show the following themes and motifs incorporated into his later poetry: his devotion to the ideal of freedom; his concern for his fellow man; his mission to ameliorate the human condition; his recognition that the artist must live unto himself and yet not wholly so; his early subscription to philosophical idealism, tempered by his belief that the mind does indeed associate out of apparent reality; his belief that man ultimately, through living the good life, will achieve spiritual haven. All of these initial characteristics mark Coleridge as a poet in the Romantic tradition and, further, provide the foundations for that which is to come. A consideration of the major minor poems, in the following chapter, will show Coleridge in a more mature, more esthetically appealing role.

CHAPTER 4

The Major Minor Poems

U NLIKE the minor poem potpourri and unlike the poems in Group II (the "Lines . . ." group), the poems in Group I (the "Eolian Harp" group), are interesting for many reasons. First of all, these poems by and large give pleasure to the reader. One of the simplest ways to convey the distinction between the minor poems and the major minor poems is to resort to Archibald MacLeish's poetic statement, "A poem should not mean/ But be." [1] Too often the poems in the potpourri and in the "Lines . . ." group contain only that which *means;* that is, there is little if any esthetic pleasure to be derived from reading them. On the other hand, the poems under discussion here which constitute the "Eolian Harp" group not only *mean* but also, in the MacLeish sense, *are.* It should be noted, however, that all of the conversation poems by definition have meaning, for this is the essential distinction between the conversation poems and, as shall be seen in the following chapter, the poems of high imagination. Nonetheless, the best of the conversation poems, in this study designated "Major Minor Poems," both mean and are. For this reason, they rise above the poems of the potpourri and the "Lines . . ." group, although admittedly they never reach the heights attained by the poems of high imagination.

I *Eolian Harp*

In consideration of the individual poems within Group I, the "Eolian Harp" itself can be read with pleasure without a redaction of the poem for meaning.[2] It is a poem which comes full circle from Eden to Eden, and yet it is in the "Eolian Harp" that Coleridge attempts to utilize his theory of the reconciliation of opposites. Obviously, this theory had not as yet been recorded in the *Biographia Literaria,* for that work was still to be undertaken. Nonetheless the tension[3] existing in the poem appears almost immediately with the advent of a beanfield in Eden. In the opening lines, a pensive Sarah, at this time Coleridge's beloved wife, reclines her cheek upon the poet's arm, in an idyllic setting, the Cot at Clevedon. This setting, permeated by the odor of Jasmin and Myrtle, emblems of "Innocence" and "Love," receives a scent wafted on the breeze which comes not from another similar flower but one "Snatch'd from yon bean-field!" (l. 10) The homely word, beanfield, connotes a different Coleridge from the trumpeting poet of the "Monodies"; the "bean-field," lowly yet sweet, carries within it the reality of an English Eden.

Although the poem's title indicates an instrument fit for gods only, the actual instrument in the poem is "that simplest Lute" placed lengthways in the casement. Here again the simplicity of the actual instrument is analogous to the simplicity and reality inherent in the beanfield image. The lines of the poem move as smoothly here as does the breeze across the lute. The stress created by a lowly beanfield in Eden gives way to another stress, that created by the analogy of the breeze caressing the strings of the lute like the hands of a lover caressing "some coy maid" who, as the yielding and strengthening song of the lute, half yields then resists the lover's importunities.

More striking than the lute-lover image is the juxtaposition of the pensive Sarah, all innocence and love, with the coy maid, who half yields, half resists. Here the stress springs from the juxtaposition of innocence with sophistication, simplicity of faith with subtlety of behavior. The stress arising from these opposite pairs may well not communicate itself consciously to the reader, but from the resultant tension stems the poem's inner dynamism. Useful to this end too is the tension created by the existence within the poem of antithetical personalities. The poet, here of course Coleridge himself, is imaginative; he gives full sway to fantasies "As wild and various as the random gales/ That swell and flutter on this subject Lute!" (ll. 42–43). Antithetical to him is Sarah, serious, orthodox, "Meek Daughter in the family of Christ!" (l. 53).

Opposite personalities in this Eden at Clevedon predicate differential reactions to the environment. For Coleridge, the wild fantasies before his half-closed eyes, conjured by the wind and flowers, here animated nature, raise in his mind's eye the question of nature's part in the larger scheme. In a microcosmic way may not all nature be similar in function to the function provided by the Eolian Harp?

> And what if all of animated nature
> Be but organic Harps diversely fram'd,
> That tremble into thought, as o'er them sweeps
> Plastic and vast, one intellectual breeze,
> At once the Soul of each, and God of all?   (ll. 44–48)

Such obstinate questionings, however, are not appropriate to the more serious-minded Sarah, who Coleridge here reveres for her simple faith; and he concludes that man's task is as simple as Micah saw it, to do justice, love mercy, and walk humbly with God. All other thoughts seem to the poet in reflection of Sarah's point of view but ". . . shapings of the unregenerate mind," (l. 55) the babblings of "vain Philosophy." Obviously the two antithetical projected personalities represent two antithetical approaches to God: the one, Coleridge's semi-skeptical, unorthodox; the other, Sarah's traditionally acquiescent accepting on the basis of faith alone, and therefore orthodox. The poet, naturally inclined to flights of fancy, to questioning and wandering in search of a rational explanation, finally gives way to Sarah's point of view, that is, to an acceptance of the necessity for faith *in* and feeling *for* God. The poet speaks through the following lines in affirmation of this:

> For never guiltless may I speak of him,
> The Incomprehensible! save when with awe
> I praise him, and with Faith that inly feels;
> Who with his saving mercies healed me,
> A sinful and most miserable man,
> Wilder'd and dark, and gave me to possess
> Peace, and this Cot, and thee, heart-honour'd Maid!
>   (ll. 58–64)

The reconciliation of both outer and inner opposites, that is, both those of image and those of personality, occurs in the final lines of the poem when the poet thanks Sarah in his heart for reaffirming in him the efficacy of faith in and feeling for God; thus the mind comes to rest in that same Eden wherefrom it had departed, and all is, for the moment at least, reconciled.

Perhaps a poem should indeed not mean but be, and, to this point, the "Eolian Harp" is a true poem. The images and the personalities are striking enough to deserve approval from a purely belletristic standpoint. But the poem has meaning also. The reconciliation taking place at the end of the poem occurs for the moment but not forever. God is still *Incomprehensible,* and the poet is still guilty when questioning instead of accepting on faith. When Coleridge is fundamentally Coleridge, he is not Sarah; nor can he resort with any conviction to her approach, either to God or to life. Coleridge is ever a philosopher as well as a poet. The reconciliation occurring at the end of the poem is not a final one; it does not go beyond the limits of the poem. The philosophical quasi-religious questioning of lines 44–48 is habitual with Coleridge's mind and will become more intense and more significantly so as time goes on, and the Coleridge "metaphysic" unfolds. In the poem, Coleridge has succumbed to the simple beauty of this English Eden, as he succumbs for the moment to Sarah's simple acceptance of life. In the poem, Coleridge seems himself as guiltless only when he accepts, along with Sarah, God on faith without attempting a rational explanation of his own method. But the Coleridge "metaphysic" would never have developed if such were the final solution for the poet. A life of simple faith lived in idyllic Clevedon, although romantically appealing and unquestionably innocent, would scarcely provide enough intellectual or moral challenge to a man of Coleridge's peculiar talents. Here Coleridge departs radically from the solution advanced by Wordsworth.

II   *Reflections on Having Left a Place of Retirement*

Ever pushing toward a greater synthesis, "Reflections on Having Left a Place of Retirement" bears out Coleridge's reluctance to accept such earthly, although seemingly Elysian, isolation as the *final* solution.[4] This poem, written after he had left Clevedon, illustrates the lack of external reconciliation effected by the solution advanced in the "Eolian Harp." In "Reflections . . ." Coleridge sees the cottage at Clevedon and the surrounding countryside as ideal in external beauty, perfect in its potential for eliciting communion with God. Here God is omnipresent; here in the shoreless ocean, ". . . the whole World/ Seem'd *imag'd* in its vast circumference." Here, "It was a luxury,—to be!" (ll. 36–42). Coleridge, the poet, seems always content to *be,* but Coleridge, the moral philosopher, must not remain in this idyllic place:

> . . . Was it right,
> While my unnumber'd brethren toil'd and bled,
> That I should dream away the entrusted hours
> On rose-leaf beds, pampering the coward heart
> With feelings all too delicate for use? (ll. 44–48)

He therefore leaves the cottage and country ostensibly ". . . to fight the bloodless fight/ Of Science, Freedom, and the Truth in Christ" (ll. 61–62). Here the tension so essential to Coleridge's poetic theory is created by conflicting desires within the man himself. The wish to remain amidst beauty wherein God is mirrored stands in opposition to the compulsion he feels to go forth in the cause of suffering humanity. The internal reconciliation is accomplished in the last lines of the poem when the poet permits his spirit to recall Clevedon, thereby to relive those exquisite moments so necessary to spiritual rejuvenation, while he in actuality continues in the bloodless fight to ameliorate the suffering of humanity. Again, this reconciliation is not a final one. Coleridge, the poet, in opposition to Coleridge, the philosopher, will continue to be in conflict throughout his life, a conflict in which ultimately the poet makes way for the philosopher.

"Reflections . . ." per se, although not so striking in imagery as is the "Eolian Harp," still has much to recommend it in this respect. Although the traditional myrtle and jasmin again appear, the poet's eyes and ears reproduce real scenes, and the imagery is sharply effective, as the following example affirms: "Bare bleak mountain speckled thin with sheep;/ Gray clouds, that shadowing spot the sunny fields;/ And river, now with bushy rocks o'er-brow'd" (ll. 30–32). The impression left with the reader that the cottage and its surroundings are inestimably lovely, quiet, and peaceful is a paramount one, while the dead lines: "I therefore go, and join head, heart, and hand,/ Active and firm, etc." (ll. 60–62), do not move the reader at all, except to make him wonder if the move from Clevedon for the cause of humanity was a necessary one.

Both poems show Coleridge turning away from the soothing panacea which nature provides into the complexities of nineteenth-century life and thought. Although the "Eolian Harp" leaves the poet in the Eden of nature, his spirit ranges abroad into more complex paths before returning; in the poem "Reflections . . . ," the poet leaves the natural Eden in the final lines of the poem because Eden is not yet meant to be. Variations on this same theme occur from time to time in Coleridge's later poetry.

III *This Lime-tree Bower . . .*

These two poems with their indications of a sharpening of visual imagery point to the highly successful imagery of the third poem in Group I, "This Lime-tree Bower My Prison." [5] Almost everyone knows the circumstances which initiated the poem's composition: how Coleridge was kept from joining Charles Lamb and his sister in their walk through the lovely countryside by an injury to his foot; how to Coleridge this enforced rest at home seemed a catastrophe; and how, out of this experience, he created a splendid poem within which he achieved a state of mind not only reconciled to, but victorious over, these circumstances. The poet's first thought expressed in the opening lines is one of extreme desolation: "Well, they are gone, and here must I remain,/ This lime-tree bower my prison! . . ." (ll. 1–2). This dejection arises from the feeling that he has missed forever the beauty unfolding before the eyes of his friends who "wander in gladness" through scenes which he himself recalls as having seen before and now sees again in memory (ll. 3–20). In his meditation, he not only sees these scenes again, but also envisages his friends emerging happily into open vistas which include perhaps ". . . some fair bark." His friend, Charles, appears to him in his mind's eye as happiest of the walkers, for Charles has lived not only in the midst of a bustling, dirty city, but also in the midst of great personal sorrow and trouble; the beauty of the natural scene should therefore wash out both physical squalor and mental anguish. In the wish that such be the case, Coleridge asks that the landscape become more beautiful, more illuminating and illustrative of spirituality, for the sake of this beloved friend (ll. 28–43). As the poet's heart opens not only to thoughts of remembered natural beauty, but also to thoughts which mitigate for the happiness of his friend, the lime-tree bower becomes not a prison but a place of consummate beauty: "A delight/ Comes sudden on my heart, and I am glad/ As I myself were there!" (ll. 43–44). At this instant also, he awakens to the specific beauties of the bower. His eye minutely traces this miniature, yet eloquent, loveliness:

> . . . Nor in this bower,
> This little lime-tree bower, have I not mark'd
> Much that has sooth'd me. Pale beneath the blaze
> Hung the transparent foliage; and I watch'd
> Some broad and sunny leaf, and lov'd to see
> The shadow of the leaf and stem above
> Dappling its sunshine! . . .   (ll. 45–51)

The poet's eye continues to trace this proximate beauty, to see in the near evidence of the far—to see, as it were, the all in each. The conclusion reached is, "That Nature ne'er deserts the wise and pure;/ No plot so narrow, be but Nature there" (ll. 60–61), which results not only in his acceptance of the lime-tree bower as a place of beauty and peace but also in his confirmation of the existence of beauty in the part, in each, as well as in the whole, in all. Man, the poet, must seek and find beauty in this way and thus ". . . keep the heart/ Awake to Love and Beauty!" (ll. 63–64). This entire mental construct also allies Coleridge with the Romantic tradition.

Although the poem may be significant externally for this alliance, the poem is significant internally for the accuracy of its natural description. Coleridge himself knew and recognized this inherent virtue. In the last lines, he speaks of the creeking flight of a rook, heard by him and, he hopes, heard by Charles too. In a footnote to the text he remarks that, ". . . Bartram had observed the same circumstance of the Savanna Crane," a notation which indicates the poet's interest in description.[6] No less effective than the creeking rook are the allusions to the silent wheeling bat and the solitary humble-bee singing in the bean-flower.

The poem contains a universality which serves to make it stand paramount among the pre-*Lyrical Ballad* poems as a study in paradox and in the reconciliation of opposites. The title itself is paradoxical. The lime-tree bower connotes singly a place of green vitality; the prison connotes singly a place of darkness and death. In addition, minor reconciliations abound in the poem. Few there are, for example, who have not at one time or another been "bereft of promis'd good" and sought therefore to reconcile themselves to such an unfortunate state. To find joy in the midst of disappointment by seeing signs of the universal in the particular; that is, to find the beautiful missed in the beautiful found, is not only a fact of the poem, but is also another instance of the Coleridge "metaphysic" enacted. In this fashion, the bower undergoes a metamorphosis, brought about by the will of the poet opening his mind and heart to the natural beauty around him. The circle from prison to Eden is analagous to the move from dejection to joy.

The tension within the poem emanates on the one hand from the attraction provided by the "wide landscape" and glorious vistas seen in reality by Coleridge's friends, and, on the other hand, from the attraction provided by the loveliness inherent within the bower seen directly by the poet himself. Beauty inherent within the bower is thus emblematic of beauty everywhere. In this conclusion lies the reconciliation of the apparent opposites as well as the resolution of paradox. Each and all suffice to indicate one central harmony, even as the creeking rook has its place as it crosses ". . . the mighty Orb's dilated glory" (l. 72). The catalyst to this reconciliation is love: first Coleridge's love for Charles which overcomes his own disappointment at not being able to revisit the "wide landscape," and brings about delight that Charles may see such beauty directly; second, love in his heart which causes him to bless the creeking rook as it wings its way through the dusky air (ll. 68–76), holding a charm for Charles ". . . to whom/ No sound is dissonant which tells of Life" (ll. 74–76). More so than the "Eolian Harp," more so than "Reflections . . . ," this poem stands as poetry as such. It *is* at least as much as it *means*. Coleridge, in his attention to the apparent realities in nature, in his accurate delineation of them, is here more the poet than the moral philosopher. Still the poem does contain within it some of the ideas which were to culminate eventually in that body of concepts called in this study the Coleridge "metaphysic": the belief that each finite thing has the capacity to reflect the infinite; the belief that love is quintessential to the good life; and the belief that a reconciliation of head with heart, of knowledge with feeling, is necessary to man if he is to realize that third and final quality, magnitude of soul.

IV *France: An Ode*

The next three poems may be considered properly as major minor poems also. The first two are more topical in nature, and one of these more esthetically appealing than the other. The third poem might well serve as a bridge to the poems of high imagination, for it is in many respects the most magical of all. Of a topical nature, "France: An Ode," was well received by the public and derived a large measure of its popularity from its empathy with the current political trend.[7] Coleridge, ever an advocate of freedom, had been in deep sympathy with the French revolutionists, as had so many other Englishmen of the time, and had, like those others, become incensed by what he considered a violation of faith by the French. Specifically, Coleridge withdrew his support when France invaded the republic of Switzerland, and it was out of this act that the poem grew. In the poem, Coleridge in emphatic poetic statements decries the betrayal of freedom by tyranny. He relates that the "spirit of divinest Liberty," always to him a holy spirit, has still his utmost devotion, but that France in her current actions has betrayed this spirit and cloaked her assault under nominal wreathes of glory. In Stanza IV, France is addressed scathingly as follows:

> Oh France, that mockest Heaven, adulterous, blind,
>   And patriot only in pernicious toils!
> Are these thy boasts, Champion of human kind?
>   To mix with Kings in the low lust of sway,
> Yell in the hunt, and share the murderous prey;
> To insult the shrine of Liberty with spoils
>   From freemen torn; to tempt and to betray?   (ll. 78–84)

Stanza V laments the fruitless search for the realization of liberty: to attempt to realize the ideal of liberty is to destroy it. Liberty in fact is not commensurate with governments, for governments are assailed by the conflicting desires and demands of many individuals, as the following lines affirm:

> The Sensual and the Dark rebel in vain,
> Slaves by their own compulsion! In mad game
> They burst their manacles and wear the name
>   Of Freedom, graven on a heavier chain!   (ll. 85–88)

In a sense, Liberty is written on the insubstantial wind and there has its sway. Liberty is for the individual, but only as a mode of thought, an ideal, expressed consummately in nature, yet never realized in the active life of men: "Yes, while I stood and gazed, my temples bare,/ And shot my being through earth, sea, and air,/ Possessing all things with intensest love,/ O Liberty! my spirit felt thee there" (ll. 102–5). Indeed, the thought expressed in the *Ode* seems to demonstrate how far Coleridge has moved away from the dream of an impossible utopia in fact (such as Pantisocracy) toward the dream of a possible utopia in thought.

V *Fears In Solitude*

"Fears In Solitude" is also somewhat topical in nature.[8] The political state of England in 1798 incorporated within it the fear of invasion. Out of this possibility grew the poem. The theme of the poem is fear, fear for the passing of the good life should such an invasion take place, and fear on Coleridge's part that many English men and women were unwittingly, though steadily, adding to the possibility that such an invasion might well be imminent. In the poem, the "good life" is equated with the lives led by simple men who live surrounded by the beauteous forms of nature. These men, far from the cries of those countrymen who clamor for war, are settled among the sweet influences of rural life and find, "Religious meanings in the forms of Nature!" (l. 24). If such men be stricken with fear, their fear rises not from their own natures but, rather, from the knowledge of those crimes against humanity committed by their countrymen.

Coleridge empathizes completely with these simple men. He muses over the state of England and over her dire prospects should the people continue in these thoughtless ways. Not only at home but also abroad are Englishmen wont to spread a pestilential plague:

> . . . Like a cloud that travels on,
> Steamed up from Cairo's swamps of pestilence,
> Even so, my countrymen! have we gone forth
> And borne to distant tribes slavery and pangs,
> And, deadlier far, our vices, whose deep taint
> With slow perdition murders the whole man,
> His body and his soul!   (ll. 47–53)

And at home, in England, the world becomes a market place, "Contemptuous of all honourable rule,/ Yet bartering freedom and the poor man's life/ For gold, as at a market!" (ll. 61–63).

In the final lines, Coleridge turns his thought to his own individual situation, that is, to his beloved Stowey with its peaceful vales and hills, to his ". . . own lowly cottage" where his wife and child dwell in peace (ll. 225–26). His return to his wife and child in thought parallels his return to them in actuality, for he comes from the surrounding countryside, where he has given vent to his fears for his country's safety, to his own simple cottage. The walk has proved beneficial in alleviating his rancor and in preparing his heart for communion with his own kind. He returns, as the lines affirm, ". . . grateful, that by nature's quietness/ And solitary musings, all my heart/ Is softened, and made worthy to indulge/ Love, and the thoughts that yearn for human kind" (ll. 229–32).

Like "France: An Ode," the topical nature of the subject matter of "Fears In Solitude" makes the poem less timely for today, and yet there are war lovers and corruption in every age, and there are men who deplore that this is so. The most serious charge that can be brought against the poem is that it is not poetry as Coleridge generally conceived poetry to be. In fact, it is the one poem in this group that may *mean* but *is not*. Coleridge recognized that this was true and said so in a note to the poem in which he called it, ". . . a sort of middle thing between Poetry and Oratory." [9] Like "France" too, the poem suffers from a lack of "heart." The former is, of course, more impassioned than the latter, but still, despite the poet's obvious sincerity, neither poem rises to a height close to the Olympus of the poems of high imagination.

VI *Frost At Midnight*

This statement would not be valid in a consideration of the third poem in this chronological trilogy, "Frost At Midnight." [10] In this poem, there is no concern for politics or international relations. The poem is, rather, a description of the poet's sense of solitude and his awareness of the comfort to be gained by being close to nature, a theme observed in these earlier poems. The opening lines of "Frost At Midnight" are given over to a description of the deep silence which surrounds the poet as he muses virtually alone, his sleeping infant son by his side, in the firelit room. The fire has burned low in the grate, leaving only a thin, blue flame (called the "stranger") hovering above it. This "stranger" is the "sole unquiet thing" in the room (ll. 1–16). It is a phenomenon which is supposed to indicate the approach of a friend. Here this "stranger" not only is at the moment companionable to Coleridge, but also serves to remind him of other rooms, other fires, other "strangers." Reminiscences of dearly remembered scenes from his school days serve in turn to remind him of the loneliness of his own youth (ll. 23–38). At this point, his thoughts turn to his sleeping son and to his realization that the babe, unlike the young Coleridge, will be raised in the midst of nature's loveliness. He shall therefore never have to seek surcease from loneliness in a flickering low fire:

> My babe so beautiful! it thrills my heart
> With tender gladness, thus to look at thee,
> And think that thou shalt learn far other lore,
> And in far other scenes! For I was reared
> In the great city, pent 'mid cloisters dim,
> And saw nought lovely but the sky and stars,
> But *thou,* my babe! shalt wander like a breeze
> By lakes and sandy shores, beneath the crags
> Of ancient mountain, and beneath the clouds,
> Which image in their bulk both lakes and shores
> And mountain crags: . . .   (ll. 48–58)

All seasons, the poem continues, whether heat of summer or frost of winter, shall be sweet to the boy, and he shall be less alone, because of his proximity to nature, than had been his father before him.

The poem displays Coleridge's skill at juxtaposing opposites in order to achieve unity. The frost is juxtaposed with the fire; the beauteous freedom of nature with the cloistered dimness of the city; the "trances of the blast" with the "secret ministry of frost"; the lonely city-cloistered boy with the sleeping babe, potentially free in nature. Most of these pairs of opposites are developed to a much greater extent than can be seen in an initial reading of the poem. For example, the frost–fire pair expand in the following fashion: the frost outside on the window with the fire inside on the hearth are both equally mysterious in their subtle natural machinations: "The Frost performs its secret ministry,/ Unhelped by any wind" (ll. 1–2). The fire is equally unexplainable. Its fluttering nature seems to the poet to ally itself with his own unexplainable nature, a point to which the following lines give support:

> Methinks, its motion in this hush of nature
> Gives it dim sympathies with me who live,
> Making it a companionable form,
> Whose puny flaps and freaks the idling Spirit
> By its own moods interprets, every where
> Echo or mirror seeking of itself,
> And makes a toy of Thought.   (ll. 17–23)

Still another pair of opposites juxtaposes the peaceful, cradled infant with the cabined, cribbed, and confined schoolboy. The confined schoolboy had for his teacher the "stern preceptor" of Christ's Hospital School, while the now sleeping infant can anticipate as teacher Nature and God manifest through her various forms. The artistic tension created by this series of antithetical images creates for "Frost At Midnight" a place comparable to that earned by "This Lime-tree Bower My Prison." Although no conversation poem can rightly be said to stand equally with the poems of high imagination (or at least on equal footing with the three great poems within this category), certainly "Frost At Midnight" and "This Lime-tree Bower . . ." both have within them that quality of heart so essential to these latter poems. Because of this quality, and because of the striking effectiveness of their imagery, these poems can be said to be the true harbingers of Coleridge's greatest poems, the poems of high imagination.

The Great Poems: The Poems of High Imagination

OF all the poems Coleridge wrote, three are beyond compare. These three, "The Ancient Mariner," "Christabel," and "Kubla Khan," produce an aura which defies definition, but which might properly be called one of "natural magic."[1] Subordinate to these three great poems, yet allied to them by virtue of some of their same qualities and characteristics, are two other poems, namely: "The Ballad of the Dark Lady" and "Lewti." All five poems have in common an emphasis upon the supernatural supernatural, and, although each is markedly different from any other in at least one respect, all have the distinction of being remote from the "beanfield" of ordinary living while at the same time being intimately involved with that world considered by the Romantics to be the *really real,* that is, the world of imagination.

I *The Rime of the Ancient Mariner*

Taken in the order and emphasis suggested, "The Rime of the Ancient Mariner" is the first of the five to want consideration.[2] It is undoubtedly a fact that this poem is as well-known as any poem in the English language, for it is read at all educational levels from the grade schools to the graduate universities. The poem is one of virtually infinite paradox. As such, it lends itself to a reading at almost any level chosen, that is, from a simple adventure narrative to a complex study of the nature of good and evil. No discussion of the poem can hope to be invitingly fresh. This is not to say that the last word on the poem has been uttered, but rather that the last word on the poem seems to elude utterance.

Certainly the poem is one profoundly involved with the theme of love as an efficacious power. But this conclusion can be reached only through a thoughtful consideration of the text of the poem itself. In Part I of the poem, an Ancient Mariner, imbued with the mesmeric power of the eye, stops a Wedding Guest who is scurrying to do his duty as "next of kin" to the bridegroom. The Mariner compels the Wedding Guest to listen to a tale not only of high adventure, but also of woe. The Wedding Guest is fretful and impatient, desirous of getting on with the festivities and merriment. Up to here, the student or reader is in no trouble. The narrative is clear and seemingly unclouded (ll. 1–20). It is not, however, sufficient in and of itself to stand as the ultimate in meaning. It should be noted that the Wedding Guest stands in these lines as a man concerned with externals, that is, with the merriment and festivities of the occasion rather than with the more sacred implications of the marriage ceremony. In this sense, the Wedding Guest is demonstrating a superficiality in his mode of living. Under the hypnotic spell of the Mariner, however, the Wedding Guest has to set aside the considerations of the workaday world, of the "beanfield" so to speak, and attend to the Mariner's story.

The Mariner then begins to tell of a voyage which began propitiously but proceeded disastrously. On this voyage, the ship, the crew, and he set forth in fair weather, only to become endangered by floating icebergs (ll. 21–65). The situation appeared perilous until, like an emissary from heaven, an Albatross flew into sight. At the appearance of this bird, representative of land, here symbolic of the known world, "The ice did split with a thunderfit;/ The helmsman steered [them] through!" (ll. 69–70). The bird seems, therefore, to be a symbol of good to the icebound mariners.

Throughout the account given by the old mariner, the Wedding Guest has from time to time interrupted (ll. 31–32; 37–38; 89–91). The interruptions of the Wedding Guest stand within the poem for the interruptions of a world not imaginative but, rather, materialistic. The Wedding Guest, here concerned with the more superficial aspects of the festive occasion, quite appropriately represents the world of Understanding as Coleridge later defines it.[3] In effect, the Wedding Guest is hostile here to the things that matter, that is, to the "really real" experiences of the Mariner. In addition, the Wedding Guest, in his insensitivity, thinks that the Mariner is possessed of an evil spirit (I. 80).

At this point in the Mariner's account, the act of the Mariner merges in its insensitivity with the initial attitude of the Wedding Guest, for the Mariner tells of *unthinkingly* shooting the Albatross. The rest of the poem depends for its motivation upon this thoughtless act. From this act redound a host of implications not only for the narrative itself, but also for the meaning of the poem. First of all, at the narrative or "story" level, the crew become involved. They believe initially that the slaying of the bird will serve to militate against them all. "Ah wretch! said they, the bird to slay,/ That made the breeze to blow!" (ll. 95–96). Then, with changing circumstances seemingly propitious to the voyage, they do an about face and commend the Mariner for the act, " 'Twas right, said they, such birds to slay,/ That bring the fog and mist" (ll. 101–2). These four lines are important, for they indicate the degree of the crewmen's participation in the sin. The Ancient Mariner has unthinkingly slain the bird, but the mariners participate consciously in the guilty act. They are, as it were, accessories after the fact. For this reason, they will not live to see the end of the voyage, while the Ancient Mariner will live on, though bound to do penance for as long as he lives. What all of this means must await further explication. It is justifiable, however, to ally the crewmen at this point with the Wedding Guest in terms of their irresponsible actions. As the Wedding Guest was concerned with externals, so they too are similarly concerned. The Wedding Guest frets at restraint; he wants to join the merry din of the external world, the wedding festivities. The crewmen approve the slaying of the Albatross when external circumstances appear favorable and disapprove the act when these circumstances appear unfavorable.

In the text of the poem itself now, the implications of the Mariner's act are spelled out. The ship forges ahead into a "silent sea" where the predicament of the crew becomes worse and worse. They become parched with thirst in the midst of rot and rotten things. In consequence, they dream of a spirit who seems to have followed them from an antithetical climate, "From the land of mist and snow" (l. 134). By this time, the reader is wholeheartedly absorbed in the tale and has forgotten the Wedding Guest and the world of the material which he signifies. The reader has willingly suspended disbelief for the moment and has entered into the poetic experience. From here on, the tale itself is totally absorbing. The tale continues as the Mariner tells of the effects of the dream upon the crew. It seems that they have viewed this spirit from the land of mist and snow as one bent on revenge. Seeking a way to redeem themselves, they look upon the Mariner as a scapegoat and hang the Albatross around his neck; in this fashion they assuage their own guilty feelings by exacting penance of him who killed the bird. Their act will not, however, suffice to absolve them, for they too are now active participants in the crime. Indeed, the degree of their guilt, because it was conscious and motivated by circumstances, is far greater than that of the Mariner.

In Part III, the crewmen begin to pay the ultimate penalty; their plight becomes desperate: "Each throat/ Was parched, and glazed each eye./ A weary time! a weary time!" (ll. 143–45). At this point in the narrative, the Mariner beholds, as does the crew, a remarkable phenomenon. A shape appears on the horizon; first seeming a speck or mist, the object races toward the becalmed ship, takes form, and appears to be a skeleton ship moving in defiance of the natural elements of wind and water. There is no wind to carry her to the mariners and there is no hull to keep out the water, yet she forges ahead coming closer and closer to the becalmed ship. From the Mariner's glittering eye, to the dreamed-of-spirit, to this obviously unnatural skeleton ship, the transition from the natural to the supernatural has taken place. In support of this point, two ghastly figures form the crew of the phantom vessel: Death and Life-in-Death, the latter a woman described in garish terms:

> *Her* lips were red, *her* looks were free,
> Her locks were yellow as gold:
> Her skin was white as leprosy,
> The Night-mare LIFE-IN-DEATH was she,
> Who thicks man's blood with cold.   (ll. 190–194)

The implications of decadent living, of thoughtless engagement in and treatment of that which should matter significantly to mankind, are obvious in this image. She is the prostitute prototype with her painted and powdered countenance, her hoyden manner, her "free looks." Coleridge may well have meant to suggest in her another mode of irresponsible behavior. Just as the Ancient Mariner in one thoughtless act has brought destruction, and as the crewmen in their capricious behavior add to it, so she by her mode of behavior sows continual destruction. The Mariner's love for the bird, one of God's creatures, was insufficient in awareness; the crewmen's love for their fellow man was insufficient in compassion; her love is simply insufficient per se. Of course she is not real, but neither is the mode of love she signifies. Like the Wedding Guest, she is superficial, thoughtless, a shadow creature; unlike him, the degree of her irresponsibility is far deeper.

As the phantom ship draws nearer, the crewmen see the unholy two, Death and Life-in-Death, gleefully engaged in casting lots for the ship's crew and for the Mariner. She wins the latter. As she shrieks, "I win, I win," one after another the other crewmen drop to the deck, dead.[4] As their souls depart, they "whiz" past the Mariner in recapitulation of the sound made by his crossbow when he committed the act which wrought this havoc. Disorder and sorrow mark the close of Part III.

The next part opens with an abrupt return to reality as the Wedding Guest interrupts the Mariner in fear that the Mariner too is as dead as are the crewmen. After reassurance by the Mariner that such is not the case, the Wedding Guest fades out while the Mariner continues his spellbinding account of life aboard the death ship. The tale now addresses itself to that solitary agony endured by the Mariner, an unrelieved agony heightened by his realization of some of the consequences of his act: "The many men, so beautiful!/ And they all dead did lie" (ll. 236–37). All those living are now reduced to the Mariner and a "thousand thousand slimy things." For seven days and seven nights, this wretched state continues. He tries to pray, but cannot. Something intrudes—"a wicked whisper," undefined by the poet, but probably meant to be the Mariner's own involvement with self, that which had isolated him in *spirit* from the Albatross, from his fellow man, from the creatures of the deep, as he has been isolated in *fact* on this becalmed ship. For a time, the Mariner remains surfeited with agony, motionless, suspended, the dead at his feet dead long enough to rot yet not rotting. Finally, aided by the coming of soft night, the shadow of the hull, the mellow light of the moon, the Mariner becomes *consciously* aware of beauty incarnate in the colorful water snakes that sport in the ship's shadow. In their happiness and beauty, he takes pleasure: "Blue, glossy green, and velvet black,/ They coiled and swam; and every track/ Was a flash of golden fire" (279–81). Unaware that he is doing so, he blesses them, an act emblematic of his return to consciousness of joy in God's creatures in lieu of his former consciousness of agony and self only. At this same instant, the dead Albatross, emblematic in a very complex way of man's inhumanity to man, and of man's rejection of love, drops from his neck. Here the external penance exacted of him by his fellow man is over, but internal penance remains.

Part V is involved with the matter of this penance. Release from the Albatross is concomitant with release from the silent sea, release from external isolation as well as from external penance. Immediately after the Albatross drops from his neck, the Mariner falls into a deep sleep in which he dreams of rain. Upon awakening, he finds the dream come true. He cannot for the moment believe his good fortune. In fact he believes, for the moment, that he is a spirit (ll. 288–308). At this point, a "roaring wind" too violent to be spiritual arises and assails the ship. The bodies which have lain lifeless on the deck rise up and man the ship (ll. 309–44). At this time in the narrative, the Wedding Guest again interrupts (l. 345). Such irrational happenings again cause him to register fear. For a second time, the Mariner reassures him with the statement that he himself is of flesh and blood and no insubstantial spirit. He continues his tale, relating how the ship, manned by a strange yet seemingly holy crew, pushes on. The crew begin to utter "sweet sounds," reminiscent sometimes of earthly bird songs and other times of an angelic choir, again reflective of the opposites: natural versus supernatural. The ship, the gloss indicates, gains its direction from the same spirit, native to the land of ice and snow, who has formerly been guardian of the Albatross and now is guardian of the ship.[5] Under its direction, the ship sails on smoothly until, abruptly, like a "pawing horse" it leaps forward; this acceleration is so rapid that the Mariner falls to the deck in a "swound," thereby providing the appropriate moment for two spirits to appear and discuss the Mariner's fate. One questions the other concerning the Mariner's sin, and is told that the Mariner who killed the bird loved by the polar spirit has already done penance and "more will do" (l. 409).

These two spirit voices continue to talk in the opening lines of Part VI. The subject of their discourse is the rapid pace of the ship, now directed by the spirit that loved the bird. The Mariner's awakening from his trance is concomitant with the ship's slowing down. Thus the ship returns to the *natural* world. Before the return is complete, however, the Mariner has one ghastly moment. As sole living member aboard, the Mariner is once again agonized by the curse lingering in the dead men's eyes. Again he tries to pray and cannot; again salvation comes to him through natural beauty, here the green of the ocean. Cognizance of it enables him to raise his eyes, to see his native country, the light house, and the kirk. He prays for verification that he lives: "O let me be awake, my God!/ Or let me sleep alway" (ll. 470–71). As he prays, the natural world becomes more and more one familiar to him. The supernatural world becomes more and more one familiar to him. The supernatural for one striking moment intrudes again as the spirits who have animated the dead crew begin to leave, their parting sign an ethereal light emanating from the last wave of each spiritual hand. And so they vanish. Silence sweet in impact falls upon the Mariner. In this instant, the reader hears with the Mariner the dash of oars signaling the approach of a pilot, a religious hermit, and the pilot's boy. The Mariner rejoices, believing the holy hermit will absolve him. But the natural world cannot as yet take over completely. This is evident in the distrust with which the Mariner is met. The small boat's crew are not convinced that the ship is that and nothing more. Nor are they convinced that the Mariner is a mariner and nothing more. As they push toward the ship, it whirls dizzily around and sinks. The Mariner, the one living soul, is hauled aboard the small boat by its apprehensive crew. The Pilot, terrified at these strange happenings, falls into a fit; the Hermit prays; the Pilot's boy laughs crazily saying: "'Ha! ha!' quoth he, 'full plain I see,/ The Devil knows how to row'" (ll. 568–69). Finally, the small craft reaches land, and the Mariner steps out upon his native soil. The Hermit, after reassurance that the Mariner lives and is no fiend, hears his compulsive confession. With these events, the return to the natural world is complete.

From that day forward, the Mariner, when brought face to face with a certain type of man (one like the Wedding Guest), feels a compulsion to confess his crime and its grim consequences. This is his eternal penance, one of conscience seeking to purge itself. The last twenty-nine lines of the poem contain that which the Mariner seems to have gleaned from his experience. The Mariner tells the Wedding Guest of an isolation on the sea so great that even God seemed to have left him. He tells of man's need for love and for fellowship:

> O sweeter than the marriage-feast,
> 'Tis sweeter far to me,

To walk together to the kirk
With a goodly company!   (ll. 601–4)

These lines bear out the reading that the poem is one concerned with man's rejection of love through his own irresponsible actions and his need to recapture a loving spirit for his salvation. The Mariner's recognition that the fellowship of the kirk is sweeter than the more superficial festivities of the marriage-feast is pertinent to this reading. The Mariner continues to expound what he has learned, namely that the efficacious power of love has brought about the act of prayer, and that he that prays best, loves best, and such love is universal. Because it is, it must be extended to all God's creatures, great or small. In this fashion must man's love extend throughout the world.

It seems then, in conclusion, that the poem is somewhat more than the facetious comment holds, a treatise on the prevention of cruelty to albatrosses. The poem transcends the particular to emphasize the universal: the necessity of awareness of and commitment to love, if man is to rise above the world of the "beanfield," that is, to rise above the world of the mere Understanding. In this fashion, the poem can best be understood as an expression of the efficacy of love. The Mariner, in this reading, is first encountered as a man representative of the wilfulness and selfishness of mankind in general. The Mariner's sin is one of selfishness, although an unaware selfishness. The Mariner, at the outset, is a being who is experienced, worldly, corrupted, and thereby set in opposition to the Albatross who is unworldly, natural, hence uncorrupted. The Wedding Guest, like the crew, is initially the same kind of man as was the Mariner at the outset of the poem. The crew share in, and add to, the Mariner's guilt, while the Wedding Guest is portrayed initially as a man concerned with the superficial aspects of beanfield-living. The Mariner learns through direct experience; the Wedding Guest leaves, at the end of the poem, to rise next morning a sadder and a wiser man. He has learned, however, vicariously, that is, through hearing the Mariner's tale. In a sense, the poem is an exegesis of the significance of man's will. Man may consciously elect to be aware and hence to do good through his awareness, or man may, through lack of awareness, commit crimes which have an inestimable effect upon himself and his associates. Not every human being is of this kind. For this reason, the Mariner knows the man to whom he must relate his story. The Wedding Guest was of this number, a somewhat insensitive, superficial entity. At the outset of the poem, the Wedding Guest was similar to the Mariner at the outset of the voyage, a man concerned with superficialities. As the Mariner is changed by his experience, so the Wedding Guest is changed by the tale (ll. 622–25). A full complement of love in the soul would have made both conversions unnecessary.

Structurally, the poem is one of opposites. The natural world of the kirk, the Hermit, the Wedding Guest, stands in opposition to the supernatural world of the spirit who loved the bird, to the specter bark with its bizarre crew, to the Mariner's strange powers, to the animated crew who man the ship, and to the movement of a ship becalmed. Thus the rational world of the "beanfield" stands in opposition to the irrational world of the supernatural. Textural opposites are also operative: heat opposes cold in the analogy of the parched throats to the land of mist and snow; cool opposes torrid, opposites manifest in the green water snakes and the red copper sun; wet opposes dry, manifest in the ocean and blood and the desert and parched mouths. In addition, there are the opposites within a given image: the attractive attributes of Life-in-Death, whose red lips and yellow hair jar against the horrible leprosy-white of her skin. External opposites set up tension also; witness the image of the immobile ship analogous in one respect to a painted picture, as the following lines illustrate:

> Day after day, day after day,
> We stuck, nor breath nor motion;
> As idle as a painted ship
> Upon a painted ocean.   (ll. 115–18)

Idleness and silence stand also in opposition to the roaring sounds made by the ice and the swift, erratic image of the ship when likened to a "pawing horse" (ll. 389–90).

These are but a few of the many devices used to convey the idea of deep contrast between the world of the natural and that of the supernatural. The tension thereby created not only captures the reader's interest but also provides the poem with a dynamic power as spellbinding to all who encounter it as was the Mariner's tale to the Wedding Guest. Still, no enumeration of devices, no description of action, no interpretation of meaning can evoke even a part of the magic evoked by the poem as a whole. Each device used adds something to the total impression, but the total is more than the sum of the technique. That which makes it so is the power of imagination brought to bear upon the world of the natural and of the supernatural to the end that these apparent opposites may be reconciled into an even more real third which is, after all, quintessential reality. For this reason, "The Rime of the Ancient Mariner" is unique in English poetry.

II *Christabel*

As "The Rime of the Ancient Mariner" exists on one level as an adventurous tale of disaster and struggle, and on still another level as a development of the idea that love is prerequisite to happiness and fulfilment in life, so "Christabel" exists as a medieval romance involving all the trappings of enchantresses, beautiful ladies, feudal barons, and their accouterments, yet at the same time as a study in ambivalent love relationships.[6] As Nethercot holds in his study, *The Road to Tryermaine*, Coleridge was probably gathering materials for "Christabel" for some three years, from 1795–98. Certainly, the first part was finished in 1798. Coleridge himself, however, cites 1797 for the date of composition, although Dorothy Wordsworth's *Journal* concurs with the former date of 1798.[7] Undoubtedly, Coleridge was preoccupied throughout this entire period with the matter and manner of demonology, demonolatry, and the like.[8] And avowedly "Christabel" itself is full of implications arising out of his concern for the supernatural and preternatural as in themselves suggestive of one explanation of the nature of evil and its machinations within the minds and hearts of the characters in the poem. Professor Nethercot has attempted to interpret the poem within the framework of traditional demonology. In a sense, he has attempted to do for "Christabel" what John Livingston Lowes in his classic, *The Road to Xanadu*, did for the "Rime of the Ancient Mariner." The reasons for Nethercot's failure to achieve comparable results is that he has devoted himself to but one aspect of the poem. "Christabel" is a great deal more than a poem superficially involved with witches, their *modus operandi*, and the sources thereof. Indeed, it has often been suggested that Coleridge's failure to finish the poem was directly owing to the depth of his involvement with the dark complexities he had permitted to rise out of the interaction of the characters. Nethercot's reading of the poem is, of course, the traditional reading, and there is much to be said in support of it. His reading is the *logical* one; that is, that the action of the poem is motivated by supernatural elements or forces and that all action and situation can be readily explained in terms of witches, lamias, and their customs and habits. The second reading of the poem might be called the *psychosexual.* This approach is upheld chiefly by Professor Roy Basler and Professor Edgar Jones.[9] In both readings, Christabel, representative of innocence, is enchanted by Geraldine, representative of the evil to which Christabel ultimately succumbs. The mode of enchantment seen in the two interpretations, however, differs radically. In the Nethercot reading, Christabel is overpowered by an external force of evil incarnate in a witch or lamia. In the Jones's interpretation, Christabel is seduced by Geraldine; hence the evil in this reading of the poem is specifically psychosexual rather than supernatural. Although the text will support both readings, neither yields an adequate explanation of the total poem. Each reading treats in the main of the relationship between Geraldine and Christabel; for this reason neither stretches far enough to encompass the other highly significant relationships. In consequence, the student of "Christabel" would be well advised to attend to the text of the poem if he wishes to evolve a satisfactory reconciliation of these two.[10]

The gist of the poem is as follows: Christabel, the beautiful, young, and innocent daughter of the rich medieval baron, Sir Leoline, has left the castle on a moonlight night in April to pray for the welfare of her lover who is far away. While praying in the moonlit wood, she hears a moan and blesses herself, thinking that some evil spirit lurks in the place. On the other side of an oak tree, she finds a lady named Geraldine, beautiful but strangely so, garbed in white, with gems that glitter in her hair. This lady tells the innocent maid a madcap tale of having been abducted by knights on horses. These men have ridden wildly through the country and have flung Geraldine down in the forest and departed with the promise that they will return. Christabel seems attracted by Geraldine's beauty, though frightened as the line implies: "I guess, 'twas frightful there to see/ A lady so richly clad as she" (ll. 66–67). After hearing the wild tale, she stretches forth her hand in answer to Geraldine's entreaty and helps the lovely lady through the wood to the castle.

The textual problems up to this point are quite clear. Christabel is undoubtedly the beloved daughter of Sir Leoline. She is, in the beginning of the poem, that and nothing more. What she is doing in the forest has been explained, though why she felt it necessary to leave the castle to pray has not been. The nature of her troubled dreams has not been revealed, but it is clear that she is restless, for she sighs as she steals along the path.

Geraldine, on the other hand, is definitely something more than she appears. And Christabel senses this, or anticipates it, as nature itself appears to do. In illustration of Christabel's awareness of Geraldine's strangeness is the former's line: "Mary mother, save me now!" (69). Seeing a beautiful lady in the midst of a forest might well evoke a prayer, but the "save me now" seems to imply perception of imminent danger. In addition to these significant initial portents of evil, Geraldine manifests a stronger sign when she feigns illness and sinks down before crossing the threshold of the castle gate. Christabel has to drag her across; once inside the gate, however, Geraldine shows no signs of malaise. Here, clearly, evil has needed the assistance of innocence to gain access to the castle. This theme will be more boldly manifest in the subsequent lines of the poem, when evil needs the permission of good in order to violate the sanctity of the heart. Although Christabel is not cognizant of all of the implications of manifest evil, she does know that all is not as it should be with Geraldine. Later, she allows herself to be "taken in." It is sufficient to point out that Geraldine displays "witchery" at the outset of the poem.

The problem posed by the character of Geraldine, however, deepens throughout the next section of the poem, and no explanation based entirely on witchcraft will suffice for every event. Ominous signs of witchcraft now appear with rapidity. First of all, once in the castle, Christabel suggests that both of them offer a prayer to the Virgin for having given them safe conduct out of the ominous wood. Geraldine begs off, saying that she is too weary to pray. Again she is lying, for they cross the courtyard without further weariness being evident. Having once entered the castle, Christabel implores that they both be silent inasmuch as her father is ill; for this reason also, she suggests that they both share the same couch. At this point the reader is again reminded that he is in the presence of evil, for Sir Leoline's dog moans angrily as the two ladies pass by:

> And what can ail the mastiff bitch?
> Never till now she uttered yell
> Beneath the eye of Christabel.
> Perhaps it is the owlet's scritch:
> For what can ail the mastiff bitch?   (ll. 149–53)

The reader is well aware that no "owlet's scritch" is the cause of the mastiff's unrest, and, were he in any doubt, the incident immediately following would banish it, for as Christabel and Geraldine pass by the dying fire in the hall, tongues of flame leap out to catch at the latter. Obviously, the flame here seeks to unite with whatever kindred elements are in Geraldine.

The stage is by this time set for the re-enactment of the fall of innocence which is to occur in Christabel's room. Stealing and sliding through the castle, the two finally arrive in the bedchamber, a room heavily gothic with its silver lamp, its curious carvings. The only light is that reflected by the moon and that emanating from the swinging, trimmed lamp. Geraldine, apparently again ennervated by her journey across the courtyard, falls down wearily. Christabel, seeing this new sign of fatigue, urges upon Geraldine a cordial made by the former's mother before she died. Within the space of a few lines, the reader encounters two distinct Geraldines (ll. 194–213). The first is a sensitive, lovely lady who asks Christabel if her mother would have pity on her, and who expresses the wish that Christabel's mother were alive and there; the second is a witchlike creature, who in strangely altered tones admonishes the spirit of the dead mother (who has appeared when summoned) to be off, in fact to leave the field free to the fell purpose of Geraldine: "'Off, woman, off! this hour is mine—/ Though thou her guardian spirit be,/ Off, woman, off! 'tis given to me'" (ll. 211–13). This second Geraldine drinks the cordial, revives, and rises imposingly to her feet: "She was most beautiful to see,/ Like a lady of a far countree" (ll. 224–25). Abruptly, however, this second Geraldine returns to the guise of the first; she speaks to Christabel of love, telling her that the spirits in the upper air love Christabel and that she herself will endeavor, in so far as she is able, to requite Christabel well.

Christabel's confusion is understandable, confronted as she has been by this dual nature of Geraldine's; like a chameleon Geraldine has shifted back and forth from a nature beautifully graceful, gentle, and quiet to one that is harsh, wild, and imperious. In this fashion, Geraldine most assuredly provides the ingredients necessary to engender ambivalent feelings in Christabel. From here on, Christabel is both attracted and repelled by Geraldine.

The rest of the poem, up to the Conclusion to Part I, elaborates in detail upon the dual nature of Geraldine. As Christabel lies down to sleep, Geraldine gazes at her, shudders, and disrobes, revealing: ". . . her bosom and half her side—/ A sight to dream of, not to tell!" (ll. 252–53). Here the reader becomes as confused as Christabel, for he is not told any more than this. It is obvious that Christabel is about to be confronted with a dramatic sight. Most critics and readers have assumed it to be a horrible one, but this is really conjecture. The M.S.W. of Coleridge reads: "Behold her bosom and half her side—Are lean and old and foul of hue." [11] Shelley is said to have run screaming out of the room upon hearing Byron recite the lines, for he had conjured a vision of eyes staring out of the breast in lieu of nipples. Whatever the sight, the MS emendations in the Ernest Hartley Coleridge edition indicate that the evil will make contact with Christabel at the same time that she comes into contact with Geraldine. In these textual variations, for example, there are several instances of lines to the effect that Geraldine will sleep either by or with Christabel and that she will be alone with Christabel during this night.[12] Geraldine, however, in the text of the poem, appears at first reluctant to effect this evil contact: "Deep from within she seems half-way/ To lift some weight with sick assay,/ And eyes the maid and seeks delay" (ll. 257–59). But then the second Geraldine takes over, steels herself "as one defied," and lies down next to Christabel, taking the innocent maid in her arms. Geraldine's reluctance to initiate the evil is once again shown in the tone of voice and look she extends ("low" and with "doleful look") when she tells Christabel that the touch of her bosom will work a spell that will exert mastery over the maid. And yet the reader is told that this same bosom will not only bring mastery of Christabel, but also that it is the mark of Geraldine's shame. This is ambiguous. Were the first Geraldine equated wholly with the second, the witch, then why does she refer to her "shame"? Geraldine is obviously not the initiator, but rather the agent, of evil. She is apparently helpless in its grip. To this point in the poem, Geraldine is drawn ambiguously. She is either the witch-lamia of the Nethercot reading, possessed by an evil spirit in much the same way that Keats' Lamia, seen through the eyes of Apollonius, is beautiful but blighted, or she is far more complex than the agent of evil explanation would suggest. It is conceivable that Coleridge meant to suggest in Geraldine two natures, good and evil, pure and sensual, reasoned and rash, broadly analogous to these same characteristics in mankind. If such is the case, then Geraldine's human qualities outweigh her witch characteristics and her brand of evil is not supernatural but, rather, psychological.[13] It is important to note that Christabel is not consciously aware of the full extent of the evil influences manifest in the second Geraldine, even though she has been puzzled throughout by the latter's rapid changes in mood. Christabel does not become fully aware of the degree of Geraldine's evil power until after the "fall."

The Conclusion to Part I, the bedchamber scene, begins by presenting a picture of Christabel, in all her innocence, praying in the wood (ll. 279–331). This image is recapitulated for the reader in order to point up the state of innocence before the fall. Christabel's gentleness, fairness, and devout countenance are dwelt upon with care (ll. 279–91). The transition from this idyllic innocence to sophistication is rapid: Geraldine, the worker of harms, the corruptor, has Christabel entranced in her arms. Christabel seems unaware of what is taking place, nor in any specific sense is the reader aware. But it is quite clear that in a short time Geraldine has been able to work evil upon the innocent maid: "O Geraldine! one hour was thine—/ Thou'st had thy will!" (ll. 305–6).

Although the specific details of the evil here wrought are not clear, still there is little doubt that the nature of the evil is sexual and that Christabel has been somewhat willing to participate. She knows, for example, "That saints will aid if men will call," and yet she has not called. In addition, she has been informed by Geraldine that physical contact with her would evoke a masterful spell, yet she has permitted Geraldine to come close to her. Part II, although written later in Coleridge's life, continues with the scene in the bedchamber the morning after the evil has been wrought. These lines give support to the belief that the evil was sexual in nature, for Geraldine, upon awakening Christabel, demonstrates that she has undergone a metamorphosis. Geraldine appears more beautiful and more voluptuous. Specifically, her breasts are fuller. It is well-known, of course, to students of demonology that witches thrive and bloom after attaining sexual satiety. It is an equally common belief that the physical act of love has restorative powers of its own which are unrelated to witchcraft per se. Christabel, however, sees and reacts to this transformed Geraldine with the words: " 'Sure I have sinn'd!' " (l. 381). She later prays that these "unknown" sins be absolved. Again, she knows in a general way that she has sinned; she seems unaware of the specifics involved.

Part II of the poem not only carries the action through to a meeting with Sir Leoline, but also develops the effect which the bedchamber incident has had upon Christabel. In addition, the reader encounters a second ambivalent relationship. If Christabel entertains feelings of ambivalence toward Geraldine and vice versa, the two have a marked precedent for them, for Sir Leoline has loved in his youth, Lord Roland, the "youthful Lord of Tryermaine," supposedly Geraldine's father. Something had occurred, some bit of gossip, to spoil the friendship between the young men:

> But whispering tongues can poison truth;
> And constancy lives in realms above;
> And life is thorny; and youth is vain;
> And to be wroth with one we love
> Doth work like madness in the brain.   (ll. 409–13)

As indicated, the keynote of this relationship was strong passion, for even though the two men had quarreled and parted long ago, some of the intensity of the love still remains in Sir Leoline's heart: "But neither heat, nor frost, nor thunder,/ Shall wholly do away, I ween,/ The marks of that which once hath been" (ll. 424–26). Because of this strong emotion, Sir Leoline transfers his affection to Geraldine: ". . . and he kenned/ In the beautiful lady the child of his friend!" (ll. 445–46). The ambivalence felt by Leoline toward Lord Roland is quite clear; in an attempt to erase past harshness, he takes Geraldine in his arms in a warm embrace. Confronted with the sight of this embrace, Christabel sees in her mind's eye Geraldine's bosom, representative to her of evil. For a brief moment, Christabel again experiences its touch and she draws in her breath with a "hissing sound" (ll. 457–59). This is the first suggestion that Christabel has been outwardly affected by her contact with evil, but the state does not last. When Sir Leoline turns to ask her why she has made such a sound, she appears once again to have returned to her pre-fall innocence. She is calm, mild, prayerful. Her answer to him, ". . . 'All will yet be well!' " (l. 472), becomes clear in the lines which state that she could not have answered otherwise in view of the powerful spell she is under (ll. 473–74). Curiously, that which prompted her mood swing from a hissing snake to a demure maid was the recollection of the time spent with Geraldine on the night her innocence was lost. Even more interesting are the lines which imply that the fall was in part a pleasant experience. Although the remembered bosom brings forth the hissing sound, the recollection of the haven found in a dream while in the lady's arms brings on the later demure state. The following lines bear out this point:

> The touch, the sight, had passed away,
> And in its stead that vision blest,
> Which comforted her after-rest
> While in the lady's arms she lay,
> Had put a rapture in her breast,
> And on her lips and o'er her eyes
> Spread smiles like light! (ll. 463–69)

These happenings are interesting. As Geraldine is always dual in nature, so Christabel has apparently become so. She now has periods when she is somewhat less than innocent. She not only seems knowledgeable with respect to Geraldine's power, but also she remembers at one and the same time the bosom cold *and* the haven found in the lady's arms. Christabel, therefore, is fraught with ambivalent feelings toward Geraldine; in this sense, she has become like Geraldine.

At this point, Geraldine, undoubtedly sensing that she has gone too far, asks Sir Leoline to send her home to her father's mansion (ll. 475–82). He refuses, saying that he has a better plan. He wishes to send Bracy, the Bard, to Geraldine's home. But Bracy begs a night's leave before setting out, and he tells a strange story by way of justifying his request. He speaks of having had a distressing dream the night before, in which he saw a dove in the wood adjacent to the castle. The dove appeared to be the one owned by Sir Leoline and named Christabel after his lovely daughter. The dove, Bracy dreamed, was being strangled by a snake of bright green hue:

> I stopped, methought, the dove to take,
> When lo! I saw a bright green snake
> Coiled around its wings and neck.
> Green as the herbs on which it couched,
> Close by the dove's its head it crouched;
> And with the dove it heaves and stirs,
> Swelling its neck as she swelled hers!   (ll. 548–54)

The implications of the dream are clear to the reader, though not at all clear to Sir Leoline. For example, Geraldine was initially described as "bright," and the snake is similarly described. The green coloring of the snake is reminiscent of the forest-green. Christabel is, of course, the dove, innocent and peaceful. A kind of allegory of the bedchamber is here enacted. The implications arising out of snake per se are those associated with the original Fall of Adam and Eve and perhaps also with the lamia motif, as Nethercot holds. The marked sensuality of the enwreathed snake; the heaving, stirring, and swelling in conjunction with the dove's breathing may well suggest the rhythmic movements of sexual relationship. Although the question may be raised in regard to whether or not this pushes the allegory too far, it is clear that Bracy wishes to stay his journey in order to search the wood, "Lest aught unholy loiter there" (l. 563).

Sir Leoline misinterprets the Bracy dream in a curiously perverse fashion. He equates the dove with Geraldine, saying, "'Sweet maid, Lord Roland's beauteous dove,'" and continues in this vein by promising Geraldine that he and her father will crush the snake. Ultimately, this is exactly what he does, for he rejects his own daughter in crushingly cruel fashion, thus bearing out his inversion of the allegory. In the meantime, however, the text of the poem reads that Leoline, believing Geraldine to be the innocent dove, kisses her fondly. She, at this point, turns her full attention upon Christabel but in a side glance: "At Christabel she looked askance!" (ll. 581, 587, 608). And she looks in such fashion not once but three times. Now it is well-known that witches do look askance at those they plague; in fact, they never look at them straightforwardly. Witches also are prone to do everything by threes. However, the lines here are ambiguous. Geraldine again illustrates her duality of nature and her ambivalent feeling for Christabel. On the one hand, she looks askance, her eyes shrunken and dull, resembling those of a snake; on the other hand, she looks at her with more of dread than malice (ll. 583–86). In addition, upon hearing Christabel emit a "hissing sound," she turns around, as the lines indicate:

> And like a thing, that sought relief,
> Full of wonder and full of grief,
> She rolled her large bright eyes divine
> Wildly on Sir Leoline.   (ll. 593–96)

Such a series of happenings proves too much for Christabel. She has fallen into a trance in which she sees nothing, yet she reflects in her own countenance the look of hate which Geraldine has sent in her direction. Once again both ladies display a duality of nature and an ambivalence.

Leoline's rejection of his daughter takes place when she awakens from the trance and requests that Geraldine be sent away. Her request enrages him and results in his ordering Bracy away immediately and in his leading Geraldine, instead of Christabel, into the hall. This latter act occurs as a result of his anger with Christabel. He believes she has been inhospitable, and he is deeply hurt, as well as angry, to think that one he loved could be so cruel. At this point, his ambivalent feelings toward Christabel are strong, as the following lines affirm:

> Within the Baron's heart and brain
> If thoughts, like these, had any share,
> They only swelled his rage and pain,
> And did but work confusion there.
> His heart was cleft with pain and rage,
> His cheeks they quivered, his eyes were wild,
> Dishonoured thus in his old age;
> Dishonoured by his only child,   (ll. 636–43)

It is essential to an understanding of the Conclusion to Part II to see this strong ambivalence. Some readers have felt that the conclusion was entirely extraneous to the rest of the poem. In fact, however, it is germane to an understanding of the poem. These lines begin with the description of a little child singing and dancing her way into her father's heart. So much does this filial-paternal love mean to the father that he must find some extraordinary way to express it. He does so by uttering harsh words: ". . .

he at last/ Must needs express his love's excess/ With words of unmeant bitterness" (ll. 663–65). The following is a commentary on this manner of expressing love: "Perhaps 'tis pretty to force together/ Thoughts so all unlike each other" (ll. 666–67). The lines suggest that perhaps it is desirable to force these strong emotions of love and hate into juxtaposition, and to ". . . dally with wrong that does no harm" (l. 669). The final lines, however, observe that such ecstasy may well be evoked only by rage and pain together, that is, only by a kind of sadistic berating of those whom one loves. And Leoline has had this problem before in his friendship with Lord Roland of Tryermaine. There too his intense love had erupted in anger and had directed him to a state of confusion: "And to be wroth with one we love/ Doth work like madness in the brain" (ll. 412–13). For they too in rage and pain had parted after bitter words never to see each other again and yet never to forget their mutual love. The Conclusion suggests that this is what has happened with Leoline and his beloved daughter. The final comment in the Conclusion suggests that such ecstasy comes only from the interaction of these strong opposites here on this earth, and grants that this can happen only in a "world of sin" (cf. ll. 670–77).

The poem as a whole shows Coleridge taking the ingredients of a medieval romance and working them into an intricate tapestry whose main theme involves a study of that powerful ambivalence which strong loves on this earth fall heir to. In the main, therefore, "Christabel" is a study of love-relationships. To recapitulate briefly, there is the "love," which might be classified as infatuation, between Christabel and the lovely lady, Geraldine; there is the love of Christabel for her lover who is far away; there is that which she holds for her father; and there is that which he holds for his friend, the "youthful Lord of Tryermaine," transferred in the poem to the supposed daughter, Geraldine; finally, though less emphasized, there is the love of Christabel and Leoline for the dead mother and wife. In three of these loves, ambivalence has been seen to distinguish the relationship: Christabel for Geraldine (and vice versa); Leoline for Christabel; and Leoline for Lord Roland.

In addition to the internal evidence presented in support of this interpretation, there is also Coleridge's own statement found in the *Notebooks*, the entry dated 1801 by Professor Coburn: "To write a series of Love Poems—truly Sapphic, save that they shall have a large Interfusion of moral Sentiment [and] calm Imagery on Love in all the moods of the mind—Philosophic, fantastic, in moods of high enthusiasm, of Simple Feeling, of mysticism, of Religion—/ comprise in it all the practice [and] all the philosophy of love" (p. 1064). It is also known that Coleridge broke into the writing of "Christabel" to write the poem, "Love," and that this poem, as Nethercot points out, raises some of the same questions as does "Christabel." [14]

A major study of "Christabel" in the light of these suggestions would be a book in itself. The final word on the poem has not been said here, but the questions raised urge any student of the poem to look deeply into the matter of love when considering theme and effect.[15] It is clear that "Christabel" is just as deeply concerned with love as is "The Rime of the Ancient Mariner"; the poem is simply another variation on one of Coleridge's most vital themes.

III *Kubla Khan*

The third major poem belonging to the poems of high imagination is "Kubla Khan." Like "Christabel," the poem is unfinished; but unlike this former poem, the circumstances of its conception are well-known to the average reader: how Coleridge had retired for peace and quiet to a lonely farmhouse, how he had taken an anodyne (opium) to induce sleep, and how he had succumbed to sleep while reading the lines from *Purchas's Pilgrimage* beginning, "Here the Kubla Khan commanded a palace to be built, and a stately garden thereunto." [16] The poet had continued to sleep for about three hours, and, upon awakening, had recorded the lines now extant until an interruption had called him away from them and made their conclusion impossible.[17] None of this account is actually relevant to an understanding of the poem; whether or not Coleridge was drugged when he wrote the poem has, however, intrigued critics almost more than have the lines themselves.[18] For this reason, perhaps, "Kubla Khan" has had several readings. Certainly one of the most enlightening of these is that which looks at the poem as a verbal enactment of the creative process. The poem, based on this interpretation, becomes unique even among

the three poems of high imagination. It is quite obviously different in some respects from either "The Rime of the Ancient Mariner" or from "Christabel."

In the fragmentary "Kubla Khan," the poet (the narrator of the
poem) sets before the reader two worlds, that of the *Imagination*
and that of the *Understanding*.[19] The latter is the world in which
all men are more or less at home; it is a world allied directly with
that of the "beanfield." The former world is, however, the world in
which the poet enters Eden, so to speak, on the "viewless wings of
poesy." Coleridge attempts in "Kubla Khan" to portray the world
of Imagination pictorially in terms of sunlit caverns and floating
pleasure-domes or, in effect, he tries to re-create creativity in action. His interest in the process of poetic creation is nowhere more
evident than in this attempt.

The poem opens with lines which indicate that Kubla Khan has
decreed the building of a pleasure dome adjacent to that spot
where Alph, the sacred river, runs "Through caverns measureless
to man" (l. 4). These caverns extend far into the ground, "Down
to a sunless sea" (l. 5). The entire terrain is, therefore, enclosed
by walls and stands as an exotic garden of ancient forests, sunny
spots of greenery, and incense-bearing trees. The place is "savage," holy and enchanted; there is within it a chasm, not an ordinary cleft, but a "romantic chasm" from which a mighty fountain
burst "momently" and whose commotion flings up "momently the
sacred river" (l. 24). This same river, which has meandered lazily
some five miles through the luxurious terrain in order to reach its
destination, sinks into the "caverns measureless to man" thunder-
ing "to a lifeless ocean," undoubtedly the "sunless sea" of the
opening stanza. To line twenty-eight, this forms the substance of
the poem.

The "caverns measureless to man," like the "sunless sea" and the
"lifeless ocean," are all remote from the actual world. Such set-
tings are unknown to the faculty of the Understanding or, more
simply, to common-sense man in the "beanfield" world. The "caverns measureless to man" are twice mentioned in order to emphasize the point that man's Understanding, that is his quantitative
abilities, his empirical readings, are insufficient. They can neither
measure the caverns, nor, in a larger sense, provide entry into this
second world. The above images all belong to this second world
of the Imagination. The image "lifeless ocean" may well mean

that man is in a world alien to that which he ordinarily views as the real world *because* he readily understands it. But it is, nonetheless, a dead world by comparison. Similarly, the next significant lines (ll. 29–30 speak of "ancestral voices prophesying war" heard by Kubla, but heard "from afar"; that is, heard outside the world of Imagination, heard from that distant land of the Understanding belonging only to the common-sense man.

The scene now shifts again to accent the pleasure-dome. Here its shadow floats midway on the waves, the allusion made real by the measured beat of the fountain's intermittent bursts, by the river's plunge into the cavern. This vision of an ideal, yet truly real, world prompts the narrator's exclamation: "It was a miracle of rare device,/ A sunny pleasure-dome with caves of ice!" (ll. 35–36). The word "miracle" above spells out for the reader the supernatural aspect of its creation. Only in the ideal world could such loveliness be realized. In these lines the accent is upon the beauty and internal reality of this pleasure-dome world of Imagination.

This vision reminds the narrator of a dream he has had in which an Abyssinian maid, a damsel with a dulcimer, played, "Singing of Mount Abora"—singing, as it were, of distant lands of enchantment and mystery. Here exists another illustration of that second world: an exotic maiden remote from the world of common sense, singing so beautifully that the narrator, in recollection of that song, knows that if he could but relive the experience of beauty thereby enjoyed, he himself could re-create the visionary pleasure-dome, not in shadow, but in song: "That with music loud and long,/ I would build that dome in air,/ That sunny dome! those caves of ice!" (ll. 45–47). He could re-create this so strikingly that those hearing it would, out of awe, be frightened by the transformation in him which such intense creativity would effect; and these listeners would then have to resort to magic to protect themselves from that which they as inhabitants of the common-sense world could never understand:

> And all who heard should see them there,
> And all should cry, Beware! Beware!
> His flashing eyes, his floating hair!
> Weave a circle round him thrice,
> And close your eyes with holy dread,

For he on honey-dew hath fed,
And drunk the milk of Paradise.   (ll. 47–54)

In further support of this reading are the terms "honey-dew" and
"milk of Paradise." These are not the food of ordinary men, nor
the fodder for a common-sense world, but are rather the nectar
and ambrosia fit for inhabitants of that world of poetic Imagination.

In this reading, "Kubla Khan" becomes clearly a recapitulation
in poetry of Coleridge's concept of the secondary Imagination,
that which transports the poet beyond the actual to the ideal
world of enchantment.[20] Nor is the poet-narrator the only one who
enters into the experience, for in "Kubla Khan" Coleridge has
done for the reader what the speaker in the poem has hoped to do
for those who would, were it possible, hear the song: bring about
that "willing suspension of disbelief for the moment" which constitutes not only poetic faith but also true reality.[21]

Technically, the poem is skilfully wrought, as are all the poems
of high imagination. The opposites within it are diverse and effec-
tively so. In tone, the poem juxtaposes quiet with noise: the silent
seas establish themselves in opposition to the cascading river; the
damsel with the dulcimer singing sweetly of Mt. Abora stands in
contrast to the woman wailing for her demon lover. Action presents its contrasts also: the peaceful, meandering river set against
the violent, bursting fountain and the flail of the thresher. Sensu-
ously, the cold of the icy caves contrasts with the heat of the
"sunny pleasure-dome." These seemingly antithetical images combine to demonstrate the proximity of the known and the unknown
worlds, the two worlds of Understanding and Imagination.

IV   *The Ballad of the Dark Ladie* and *Lewti*

There is no question but that "The Rime of the Ancient Mariner," "Christabel," and "Kubla Khan" are of major concern to students of Coleridge. Two other poems, less well-known, but having
similar implications for he who chooses to study the poems of high
imagination are "The Ballad of the Dark Ladie" and "Lewti."
These two have much in common with the major poems belonging to this category. Coleridge's preoccupation with antithetical
types of women is one case in point. On the one hand, there is the

strange woman, Geraldine, with her glances askance, her gem-encrusted hair, her wild utterances, her far-countree demeanor; in "Kubla Khan" there is the woman wailing for her demon lover; in the "Ancient Mariner" there is the Life-in-Death phantom woman who "thicks man's blood with cold." On the other hand, in opposition to this preoccupation, there is the "sweet maid Christabel," assuredly antithetical to the strange woman, Geraldine. Allied with the "sweet-maid" image is the "damsel with a dulcimer" in "Kubla Khan." Even before the poems of high imagination, this interest was made manifest in the sweet, pensive Sarah idyllic in her Cot at Clevedon. Another manifestation was the nurse portrait in the poem, "Love." [22]

Obviously, Coleridge found both types of woman, demoniacal and innocent, to hold an attraction for him. To play these opposites off against each other was a device having deep-seated origins and far-reaching implications. In "Christabel," as has been seen, he manipulates both types of women, and allows each to take on the characteristics of the other while remaining predominantly whatever her type was at the outset of the poem. In "The Ballad of the Dark Ladie," an innocent maid predominates; in "Lewti," an enchantress operates. But such is not the sole antithetical element which appears. Indeed both poems are striking in their use of contrasting elements existent not only between the two poems, but also within each. Before contrasting one with the other, therefore, it is necessary to consider each as a single entity. Once again Coleridge's preoccupation with opposites and his attempts to reconcile them are evident.

The opening lines to the "Ballad of the Dark Ladie" reveal a lovely lady sitting disconsolately upon a mossy stone awaiting her lover, a knight with a Griffin for his crest.[23] "Thrice" she sends her page up to the castle to find the knight, for he is long overdue. It is afternoon, and she has lingered in this spot all day. Finally the knight, Lord Henry Falkland, arrives. He tells the dark lady that he will take her to one of his nine castles when night falls. At this juncture, the lady shows great distress; she rants wildly about the night, the views, and the expected wedding. But the poem is clearly about more than a broken promise, as close attention to its lines reveals. Upon seeing Lord Henry, for example, the maid informs the reader that she has yielded to the knight and that he, in turn, has promised to make her his bride:

> "My Henry, I have given thee much,
> I gave what I can ne'er recall,
> I gave my heart, I gave my peace,
>   O Heaven! I gave thee all."   (ll. 29–32)

That she was the innocent maid here seduced by the experienced knight is clear. Her friends have warned her, scoffed at her, but to no avail. She trusted him, but her pledge of love was followed by her physical acquiescence in the "eye of noon" (l. 47). The "eye of noon" stands for light, legitimacy, honesty, and a host of similar meritorious qualities. But Henry's love is meretricious, as the night is meretricious. Because Henry promises her the finest of nine castles but wants to wait for night until he takes her there, she becomes distracted unto madness as the following lines affirm:

> "The dark? the dark? No! not the dark?
> The twinkling stars? How, Henry? How?"
> O God! 'twas in the eye of noon
> He pledged his sacred vow!   (ll. 45–48)

Thus she frantically rejects him, for she sees herself as innocent (although technically, of course, she is not), and she insists that Henry lead her forth to wed in the "eye of noon" only. She does not insist openly to him, but she remains firm in this resolve in her own mind. Here she turns from the reality of the common-sense world to the unreality of the world of dreams. She loses touch with the world of the Understanding. She leaves the warning of her friends, the facts of Henry's illicit proposal, and escapes into a world where men are true to those they love; indeed, where men marry those to whom commitments have been made. The following lines bear out this interpretation and also show in another way the world as it *ought* to be, an ideal world of joy and truth:

> And in the eye of noon my love
> Shall lead me from my mother's door,
> Sweet boys and girls all clothed in white
> Strewing flowers before:
>
> But first the nodding minstrels go
> With music meet for lordly bowers,

> The children next in snow-white vests,
> Strewing buds and flowers!
>
> And then my love and I shall pace,
> My jet black hair in pearly braids,
> Between our comely bachelors
> And blushing bridal maids.   (ll. 49–60)

In this dream, or ideal, state, she heaps up meritorious symbols: it is her "mother's" door; there are minstrels and sweet music; there are children in snow-white vests; there are flowers and buds and handsome young people. In short, there is an aura of sweetness and innocence wholly compatible with the sanctity of marriage. Even her "jet-black" hair is saved from the night symbolism by "pearly braids."

Every line in the poem supports the lady's innocence, and yet the poem is entitled, "The Ballad of the Dark Ladie." Clearly, she is not an enchantress, but rather the antithesis of such, the guileless, innocent maid. She is no "belle dame sans merci," but rather one who has been subjected to enchantment. In the poem, she is seen in the process of becoming disenchanted, but the process is never completed. She escapes into an ideal world of imagination.

As nearly as can be ascertained, this poem was in preparation along with "Christabel." [24] It has in common with the latter poem those external elements belonging to the medieval romance: knights, fair ladies, castles, love, passion, and a certain dreamlike quality. Internally, the theme of seduction of innocence by experience is common to these two poems. Within the "Ballad," Coleridge's habit of juxtaposing opposites is readily seen. Dark is opposed to light; experience to innocence; the knight-enchanter to the maid-enchanted; the world of reality with the world of romance; or, more accurately, the world as it is with the world as it ought to be.

In this poem, as in so many others, Coleridge takes an experience certainly not alien to the human condition and cloaks it in mystery to the end that it becomes a more powerful expression of that experience. Keats, in "La Belle Dame Sans Merci," uses the same materials but inverts the major roles. "The Ballad of the Dark Ladie," although less successful than the other poems of high imagination, utilizes the same approach to reality and the same techniques of expression. "Lewti" is another poem which, though it can scarcely be called major, demonstrates Coleridge in a similar frame of mind at a similar point in his development.[25] "Lewti" was originally intended for publication in the *Lyrical Ballads*. Again Coleridge turns to the strange lady, the enchantress, for his subject. Lewti, like Keats's lady without mercy, is not kind, for she has left the lover who in the opening lines of the poem seeks her constantly. He roams the countryside, a solitary, hoping to erase her from his mind. Like the "wretched wight" in the Keats' poem, Lewti's lover is also pale, alone, and likely to die. At least he thinks he shall die of unrequited love. His cheek compares with the whiteness of a cloud passing over the moon:

> And now 'tis whiter than before!
> As white as my poor cheek will be,
> When, Lewti! on my couch I lie,
> A dying man for love of thee.   (ll. 36–39)

Here again ambivalence appears. Although the lover begins his lament with the tale of Lewti's unkindness, he finishes with the hope that "Tomorrow Lewti may be kind" (l. 83).

The imagery of "Lewti" evokes in the reader a sense of the remote, the beautiful, the strange. "Lewti" is subtitled, "The Circassian Love-Chaunt," recalling another strange land, that of "Kubla Khan." Not by Alph but by Tamaha's stream does the lover in "Lewti" wander. The rock illumined by the moon shines through the "pendant boughs of tressy yew" as Lewti's forehead "[gleams] through her sable hair" (ll. 9–11). Although this may be an unfortunate comparison, the image serves to show how the whole scene is suffused with amber light, brought about by the moon shining through a little cloud. Such beauty exalts Lewti's lover to the hope that his love can be realized. Then, as the cloud passes from the moon and becomes in and of itself a dim, gray cloud with no inherent power to stay fixed, the lover too finds himself similarly powerless to remain fixed in his attitude toward the cruel Lewti.

The accent on clouds, themselves reflective of the elusive, the distant, the remote, the dreamlike, serves to heighten the poem's tone of isolated reverie, and to make the world of the poem strikingly different from the world of the ordinary. The world of Lewti is scarcely ordinary. Like that of "Kubla Khan," it is beautiful though remote. Even the bower where the lover believes Lewti to lie is remote, unapproachable except in reverie, as the following lines illustrate:

> I know the place where Lewti lies,
> When silent night has closed her eyes:
> It is a breezy jasmine-bower,
> The nightingale sings o'er her head:
> Voice of the Night! had I the power
> That leafy labyrinth to thread,
> And creep, like thee, with soundless tread,
> I then might view her bosom white
> Heaving lovely to my sight,
> As these two swans together heave
> On the gently-swelling wave.   (ll. 65–75)

The bower, however, has an imaginative reality far surpassing that reality belonging to the world of the Understanding.

Both "The Ballad of the Dark Ladie" and "Lewti" are about unrequited love. Both stand outside the sphere of the ordinary world of events and center on worlds either remote in time or remote in place. Both poems request and require of the reader that willing suspension of disbelief, in order that he may leave the world of common day and enter into a world more real, the world of imagination. Both poems suggest that love is efficacious, though both do so by default, for neither the knight nor Lewti is kind to beloved or lover. Both situations are projected as the beloved and lover wish them to be, and even though neither comes to pass in the poem, the implication is that were these loves to be realized, this then would be the world as it *ought* to be.

All of the poems of high imagination juxtapose the world as it appears with the world as it ought to be. None of the poems of high imagination, however, overstate the case for this visionary world. Indeed, each of the poems can be read and enjoyed for magical properties alone. But there is a logical consistency in each which adds to the magic for those who care to seek it out. This consistency is not to be found in the post-*Lyrical Ballad* poems. Among these latter, only "Dejection: An Ode" bears up under analysis, as the following chapter will illustrate. "Dejection" apprehends the "metaphysical bustard" of Coleridge's later years, something which the poems of high imagination, while not totally escaping, manage for the most part to circumvent.

CHAPTER 6

Post-Lyrical Ballads *Poems*

I *The Pains of Sleep*

THE poems of Samuel Taylor Coleridge written after the publication of the *Lyrical Ballads* are largely derivative. Translations, imitations, and the like abound. Most notable among these derivative poems is "Hymn Before Sunrise" (1802), a highly poetic expansion of a translation of Fredericka Brun's "Ode to Chamouny." The original was addressed to the German poet, Klopstock, whom Coleridge had met while traveling in Germany.[1] The best-known of the posts-*Lyrical Ballads* poems, and one which is not derivative, is "Dejection: An Ode." Another poem, also not derivative, is chronologically contemporaneous with "Dejection" although not comparable in either intensity or poetic quality.[2] This poem, "The Pains of Sleep," published in 1816, was probably composed in 1802. Coleridge referred to the verses as "dogrels," and this term seems to describe aptly the jouncing couplets, illustrated by the following lines:

> Ere on my bed my limbs I lay,
> It hath not been my use to pray
> With moving lips or bended knees;
> But silently, by slow degrees,
> My spirit I to Love compose,
> In humble trust mine eye-lids close,
> With reverential resignation,
> No wish conceived, no thought exprest,
> Only a sense of supplication;
> A sense o'er all my soul imprest
> That I am weak, yet not unblest,
> Since in me, round me, every where
> Eternal Strength and Wisdom are.[3]

These "dogrels" continue as the poet supplicates for Love and prayerfully resigns himself to it, only to be tormented by two ensuing sleepless nights. He questions why such torment has fallen to him and surmises that the tortures of sleeplessness are, in general, visited upon sinful natures only; therefore, "But wherefore, wherefore fall on me?" for, "To be beloved is all I need,/ And whom I love, I love indeed" (ll. 50–52). The poem appears to reinvoke the old techniques seen in the Juvenilia and in the earlier minor poems: rhyme for rhyme's sake and personification of qualities. It is in every way an abrupt departure from the qualities and characteristics indigenous to the poems of high imagination. The poem is in one sense more "conversational" than "imaginative," and certainly more "fanciful" than these categories allow. In consequence, the poem is much less effective than either those belonging to high imagination or those belonging to the conversation group. "Dejection: An Ode," on the other hand, though it too marks a departure from the poems of high imagination, is in effect much more successful than "The Pains of Sleep." [4] Its significance cannot be overestimated, for there is little doubt that the poem marks a critical turning point in both the poetic development and the thought of Samuel Taylor Coleridge.

II   *Dejection: An Ode*

The first known reference to "Dejection" appeared in a letter to William Sotheby, dated Keswick, July 19, 1802. [5] The contents of this letter indicate that Coleridge had been working on the poem for some months prior to this date. [6] In this letter also, Coleridge speaks of having translated about 530 lines of *The Erste Schiffer* in his attempt to ". . . force [himself] out of metaphysical trains of thought—which when [he] trusted [himself] to [his] own Ideas came upon [him] uncalled . . ." [7] He explains that the ode therefore was written during a period of deep stress which resulted from his recognition of the illusive nature of his own poetic power and from his growing propensity for "poetical prose." This latter tendency he deplored. In an attempt to crystallize this feeling, he composed "Dejection: An Ode." His words on the circumstances surrounding its creation are quoted in the following letter:

To have done with poetical Prose (which is a very vile Olio) Sickness and some other and worse afflictions, first forced me into *downright metaphysics* [and therefore away from the creation of "poetic Partridges"]/ for I believe that by nature I have more of the Poet in me/

In a poem written during that dejection to Wordsworth, and the greater part of a private nature—I thus expressed the thought—in language more forcible than harmonious—[8]

The outlines of "Dejection" are comparatively easy to follow. In the first stanza, the poet muses over the scene, a tranquil night, which is at this point disturbed only by the low moan of a lute gently raked by a soft wind. Although one might be reminded here of the scene in "The Eolian Harp," the similarities are superficial. In "Dejection" the new moon holding the old moon in her arms presages the approach of a storm as did that earlier new moon in the fifteenth-century "Ballad of Sir Patrick Spense." Coleridge used the following excerpt from that poem to initiate "Dejection":

> Late, late yestreen I saw the new Moon,
> With the old Moon in her arms;
> And I fear, I fear, My Master dear!
> We shall have a deadly storm.

The poet's own mood encroaches on this peaceful, though ominous, scene and seems a weight upon him characterized as a "dull pain" (l. 20). From here on, the poet discourses upon his inability to enter wholly into the manifest beauty of nature: he *sees* the beauty but he does not *feel* its impact. He attributes his inability to feel to two things, one external and one internal. The external, "A grief without a pang, void, dark, and drear . . ." (l. 21), is the nameless something which has happened to him. The internal is his own "heartless" mood which causes him to gaze and gaze with a totally blank eye upon nature's beauteous forms (ll. 25–30). From the knowledge that he sees but no longer feels nature's beauty comes his dejection. One is here reminded of a somewhat similar set of circumstances enumerated by Wordsworth in the opening lines of "Resolution and Independence," when he, while walking on the moors in the full glory of a bright morning, in full participation in its loveliness, suddenly becomes dejected and can no longer enjoy the beauty of the skylark, of the hare, or the natural scene as he had enjoyed them but a few minutes before: "We Poets in our youth begin in gladness;/ But thereof come in the end despondency and madness." [9] Wordsworth is saved from utter dejection by the timely vision of the leech-gatherer with his equally timely message of devotion to duty. Coleridge in "Dejection" receives no such timely message. The recognition that he seems to have lost his primal sympathy for nature causes his genial spirits to fail. Although his perception of beauty remains unimpaired, he perceives coldly and dispassionately. He has lost the power to feel, here meaning to create, to bring to nature the joy and beauty of soul so essential to a full appreciation of it:

> All this long eve, so balmy and serene,
> Have I been gazing on the western sky,
> And its peculiar tint of yellow green:
> And still I gaze—and with how blank an eye!
> And those thin clouds above, in flakes and bars,
> That give away their motion to the stars;
> Those stars, that glide behind them or between,
> Now sparkling, now bedimmed, but always seen:
> Yon crescent Moon, as fixed as if it grew
> In its own cloudless, starless lake of blue;
> I see them all so excellently fair,
> I see, not feel, how beautiful they are!   (ll. 27–38)

The control exercised in the couplets above, "grew–blue" and "fair–are," serves to emphasize Coleridge's sense of loss, the loss of imagination, of wholeness. His eye and ear are functioning, but not with the shaping power of imagination. They are functioning at the level of the understanding, that which is indigenous to the common-sense world but alien to the world of imagination. Certainly the sense of loss of power here is a departure from that which had once belonged to Coleridge as it belonged to Wordsworth. The latter had spoken in "Tintern Abbey" in 1798 of the function of the eye and ear of man in his relation to nature, saying:

> . . . Of all the mighty world
> Of eye, and ear,—both what they half create,
> And what perceive; well pleased to recognize
> In nature and the language of the sense,
> The anchor of my purest thoughts, the nurse,
> The guide, the guardian of my heart, and soul
> Of all my moral being.[10]

This concept of man's relationship to nature was one subscribed to not only by Wordsworth, but also by Coleridge, and invoked by the latter in the poems of high imagination. Now in "Dejection," Coleridge has lost the shaping power of imagination, the power to half-create beauteous forms. That inner spirit, or power, which formerly enabled him to raise ". . . a Covey of poetic Partridges with whirring wings of music, or wild Ducks *shaping* their rapid flight in forms always regular (a still better image of Verse)",[11] seems to have vanished. Indeed the "metaphysical Bustard" has taken hold of the poet ". . . urging its slow, laborious, earth skinning Flight, over dreary and level Wastes." [12] With such thoughts bearing down upon him, it is no wonder that he writes in the third stanza of "Dejection":

> My genial spirits fail;
> And what can these avail
> To lift the smothering weight from off my breast?
> It were a vain endeavour,
> Though I should gaze for ever
> On that green light that lingers in the west:
> I may not hope from outward forms to win
> The passion and the life, whose fountains are within.
>
> (ll. 39–46)

In stanza four, Coleridge continues to lament the strangulation of his soul by doubts and metaphysical speculations. He regrets also his inability to feel sufficiently to create those beauteous forms of nature and high poetry. He addresses himself in these lines to Sara Hutchinson:[13]

> O Lady! we receive but what we give,
> And in our life alone does Nature live:
> Ours is her wedding garment, ours her shroud!
> And would we aught behold, of higher worth,
> Than that inanimate cold world allowed
> To the poor loveless ever-anxious crowd,
> Ah! from the soul itself must issue forth
> A light, a glory, a fair luminous cloud
> Enveloping the Earth—
> And from the soul itself must there be sent
> A sweet and potent voice, of its own birth,
> Of all sweet sounds the life and element! (ll. 47–58)

Addressing the next lines also to Sara Hutchinson, Coleridge names what has fled his soul as *Joy,* a quality indigenous to the pure in heart, and thus belonging to such as Sara. Joy is the natural "dower" of man, enabling him to create and to participate in beauty. To Coleridge too there was a time when Joy held sway within him, when misfortunes merely seemed but were not, when hope held his soul at a buoyant and creative level. Now, however, Joy has been overcome by "affliction" which robs the poet. Each subsequent visitation of sorrow, he laments, "Suspends what nature gave me at my birth,/ My shaping spirit of Imagination" (ll. 85–86). And, as the next lines indicate, not afflictions only, but also something within himself, perhaps the growing tendency toward "abstruse research," robs him of the "natural man," that is, of his natural dower of Joy so essential to creativity. In a way, Coleridge begins to see the world as other men see it. In so doing, he, like Wordsworth, loses the ". . . gleam,/ The light that never was on sea or land,/ The consecration, and the Poet's dream." [14] But he loses it for reasons other than did Wordsworth in "Elegiac Stanzas." Wordsworth, of his own volition, set aside a "romantic" or imaginative view of life and nature and submitted to a new control, duty. With Coleridge there is no such voluntary setting aside, but rather the feeling that his own developing interests had pushed imagination aside and in consequence had stifled his ability to create. In "Dejection" he is resistant to these so-called realities, but because of an already developed habit of mind, this resistance does not hold. He attempts to rid himself of his somber mood, saying, "Hence, viper thoughts, that coil around my mind,/ Reality's dark dream!/ I turn from you, and listen to the wind,/ Which long has raved unnoticed . . ." (ll. 94–97). But the wind in "Dejection" is as violent as that wind which whipped the waves around Peel's Castle in the Beaumont painting seen by Wordsworth and commented on in "Elegiac Stanzas." The violent wind in "Dejection" is far removed from that desultory breeze in the earlier poem, "The Eolian Harp."

In "Dejection" the wind shrieks of pain, cold, evil, and loneliness. And all that Coleridge can do is pray that for Sara, the still pure in heart, the wind is but a momentary mountain storm and not really reflective of a major element in life. For him, however, nature-beautiful has become nature-terrible, the "shroud" rather than the wedding garment (l. 49). What he sees now recalls no "poetic Partridges" but rather the ". . . groans, of trampled men, with smarting wounds" (l. 112). The prayerful hope that Sara may not come to know what he has come to know, but will continue to create joy out of joy, is his expressed wish for her but not for himself. He knows that for himself both the attitude and the ability are gone. In this knowledge, he is isolated not only from Sara and nature, but also from the poetry of high imagination. There will be no more "poetic Partridges." In many respects, "Dejection" sounds the death knell of poetry for Coleridge. Those "viper thoughts" of painful reality, though admonished to be gone, never really go. In consequence, there will be no more bright-eyed mariners or lovely ladies from "far countrees" for him. As with Wordsworth, though for different reasons, the "gleam" has faded into the light of common day. From here on, matters critical, metaphysical, philosophical, theological will occupy the major portion of Coleridge's time and talent, and he will become steadily, as Milton became for a time only, a man devoted to the left hand of prose rather than to the right hand of poetry.

Many critics have looked upon this shift with jaundiced eye as evidence of Coleridge's decline. This view has become, however, outmoded, as more and more critics turn to the prose and find in it evidence of Coleridge's inordinate dedication and comparable strength of mind. Before taking up the prose works, however, the student of Coleridge should turn his attention in summary fashion only to Coleridge in his most minor, and in many respects least effective, role as dramatist. If Coleridge is ever a bad writer, it is as dramatist; and yet the fault lay not entirely with himself, but also, as shall be pointed out, in the nature of the drama at that time.

CHAPTER 7

The Dramas

THE Drama in the early nineteenth century was, for the most part, unimpressive. This is not to say that there was any dearth of drama being written, but rather that the quality of most of it left much to be desired. Harold Child calls this period ". . . the low mark of English drama in quality, together with a great increase in quantity." [1] In general, there were three major categories into which the plays of the period fell: melodramas, farces, and spectacles; tragedy, comedy, tragicomedy—all of a more serious and higher tone; and, in the final category, "poetic plays." [2] These latter, discussed by Allardyce Nicoll under the chapter heading "Still-born Drama," became the peculiar treasure of nineteenth-century Romantic poets. [3] Two groups of these poets turned their attention to this kind of drama: the first, Wordsworth, Scott, Coleridge; the second, Byron, Shelley, Keats. All of their products seem to have much in common with one another. [4]

First of all, "poetic plays" by definition read far better than they produce. All are characterized by long, declamatory speeches, a profusion of imagery, an excess of emotion—elements which seem to obscure what little action may have been intended. These traits are not accidental, however, for Romantic poets were far more concerned with pointing up philosophy or emphasizing a single passion than they were with creating a single unified dramatic effect. Thus with little or no thought to the production of the plays in an actual theater, their authors made them vehicles for thought or a selected emotion. [5] Indeed Nicoll quotes George Darley's summary remark on this subject addressed to all who wrote such plays: ". . . 'your action is nothing and your poetry everything.'" [6] It is Nicoll's point of view that the Romantics themselves were at fault for the failure of this type of nineteenth-century drama, but Watson blames the conditions of the times, of the theaters, and of the audiences themselves far more. [7] From all accounts, Watson's observations have merit. The audience was an unruly rabble composed of gossipy old women, gay blades about town, fancy ladies, orange-throwers, squabbling drunks, and hecklers. Even Nicoll agrees that these and other external circumstances, coupled with the egocentricity of the poet-playwrights themselves, served to militate against the production of quality drama. Add to all this the enormous size of the theaters, which dictated that actors' speeches be declamatory, and stentorianly so if they were to be heard at all, and one can readily see why the Romantic poets, with their interest in the internal workings of mind and heart, were not particularly successful in creating plays that lent themselves to being produced.[8] Of these poetic dramas intended for production, Shelley's *Cenci*, and Byron's *Manfred* and *Sardanapalus* are among the better known. Wordsworth's *The Borderers*, Keats' *Otho*, Scott's *House of Aspen* and *Halidan Hall*, Coleridge's *Osorio* (*Remorse*) and *Zapolya*, are usually known today only to the student of dramatic literary history. The list demonstrates, however, the involvement of the major Romantics in this dramatic genre.[9]

I *The Fall of Robespierre*

Samuel Taylor Coleridge is little known or studied as a dramatist.[10] Nonetheless, he was one of the more prolific writers of this idiom among the Romantics. His first play, *The Fall of Robespierre*,[11] written in collaboration with Robert Southey (1794), can be summarily dismissed as an abortive attempt to illustrate the two young authors' preoccupation with Pantisocratic ideas. In the play, Robespierre is portrayed as the savage tyrant who sacrifices the people's right to freedom by keeping all decision-making, all freedom of choice, under his own jurisdiction. A line of Southey's mouthed by the character Tallien advances the predominant idea of the play, that is, that the state is more than the individual will or the will of the few: "France shall be saved! Her generous sons attached/ To principles, not persons, spurn the idol/ They worshipp'd once . . ." (III. 65–67). Such thoughts on the relationship of the state to the people were to remain in Coleridge's mind throughout his lifetime. He was ever distrustful of demagoguery in any form, believing rather that the state was not only more than any one individual in it, but also more than any group of individuals. He believed, and was to advance the belief time and again, that reliance upon the will of the people might well result in chaos and anarchy. He, like so many other Englishmen of the time, had formerly believed in the ideals of the French revolution, only to turn from this belief when confronted with the practical consequences of that revolution.[12] As anticipated in the title, Robespierre and his blood-smeared cohorts fall, and Reason, in the guise of an ordered state, is restored. In this fashion, France is cast at the end of the play as the blaster of despotism and the liberator of the world, firm ever in the cause of freedom (III. 195–213).

The opening lines of the dramatic poem suffice to show the play's declamatory rhetoric, which not only marks it as belonging to a specific category, but also marks it as the heir of nineteenth-century "Shakespeareanism" and the harbinger of "Byronism." In these lines, Barrere, one influential in rallying the forces which ultimately overthrow the tyrant Robespierre, is speaking. Once the friend and supporter of Robespierre, he is seen here taking cognizance of Robespierre's tyranny and of its danger to free men:

> The tempest gathers—be it mine to seek
> A friendly shelter, ere it bursts upon him.
> But where? and how? I fear the Tyrant's *soul*—
> Sudden in action, fertile in resource,
> And rising awful 'mid impending ruins;
> In splendor gloomy, as the midnight meteor,
> That fearless thwarts the elemental war.
> When last in secret conference we met,
> He scowl'd upon me with suspicious rage,
> Making his eye the inmate of my bosom.
> I know he scorns me—and I feel, I hate him—
> Yet there is in him that which makes me tremble!
>
> (I. 1–12)

In these lines Barrere introspectively considers the nature of the tyrant's tremendous potential for action and his inherent suspicion which tends to manifest itself more and more the higher he ascends in power. The distrust engendered by tyrants in the hearts of once loyal supporter is a universal story, and yet one can readily see where the lines above lend themselves much more readily to analysis upon reading than upon hearing.

The essential difference between Coleridge's handling of the lines and Southey's appears to lie in the area of style and tone. Coleridge in Act I has Tallien address Adelaide as follows:

> I thank thee, Adelaide! 'twas sweet, though mournful.
> But why thy brow o'ercast, thy cheek so wan?
> Thou look'st as a lorn maid beside some stream
> That sighs away the soul in fond despairing,
> While sorrow sad, like the dank willow near her,
> Hangs o'er the troubled fountain of her eye.   (I. 227–32)

The pentameter line is smooth in the above, yet not metronomically so as it is in Acts II and III, attributed to Southey. The ensuing dialogue is full of rhetorical flourishes and melodramatic lines, but it is nonetheless relatively lively when compared with that of his collaborator. In addition the length of many of the speeches written by Southey far exceeds the length of those by Coleridge. Indeed Barrere's closing address to the Tribune is some fifty-three lines long.

Neither young author seems to belong to the nineteenth century. In reading *The Fall of Robespierre*, one is constrained to admit that the appearance of Wordsworth's assimilated rural diction, if it did later have an effect upon Coleridge's choice of poetic language, is more to be appreciated than reviled. A consideration of the following stilted and artificial lines written by Coleridge and spoken in the play by Adelaide bears out this point:

> O this new freedom! at how dear a price
> We've bought the seeming good! The peaceful virtues
> And every blandishment of private life,
> The father's cares, the mother's fond endearment,
> All sacrificed to liberty's wild riot.
> The winged hours, that scatter'd roses round me,
> Languid and sad drag their slow course along,
> And shake big gall-drops from their heavy wings.
> But I will steal away these anxious thoughts
> By the soft languishment of warbled airs,
> If haply melodies may lull the sense
> Of sorrow for a while.   (I. 197–208)

Throughout the play the lines lack restraint. Many of them shout deafeningly upon the reader's ears until most of the desired effect is lost. The same flaws seen in Coleridge's early poetry crop up in this dramatic poem: a profusion of classical allusion, quaint and archaic diction, declamatory style, clustered images so thick they appear mixed. An example of this latter shows up in the following lines spoken by Lengendre of Barrere:

> Perfidious Traitor!—still afraid to bask
> In the full blaze of power, the rustling serpent
> Lurks in the thicket of the Tyrant's greatness,
> Ever prepared to sting who shelters him.
> Each thought, each action in himself converges;
> And love and friendship on his coward heart
> Shine like the powerless sun on polar ice;
> To all attach'd, by turns deserting all,
> Cunning and dark—a necessary villain!   (I. 25–33)

Although it has been perhaps unnecessary to give so many illustrations, the lines quoted speak far more eloquently of the limitations of the dramatic poem, its faults and nature than can the critic. They also serve to provide some idea of what is to come, for the faults inherent in *The Fall of Robespierre* are never wholly pruned away from Coleridge's subsequent dramas.

Before considering these other dramatic poems, however, Coleridge's translations of Schiller's *Wallenstein* are deserving of mention. He translated Schiller's play in two separate parts entitled *The Piccolomini* and *The Death of Wallenstein*. While these cannot be considered in this study of his writings, they are nonetheless important. Not only did they bring Schiller's magnificence more sharply before English readers, but they also serve to demonstrate once again Coleridge's reverence for German thought and writing.[13]

II Remorse

Coleridge's next play, *Osorio*, herein considered in its rewritten form entitled *Remorse*, serves, as the title of the revision suggests, to point up Coleridge's preoccupation with a single passion or emotion. This is the only one of Coleridge's plays which was produced. The play opened at Drury Lane Theatre on January 23, 1813, and closed twenty-eight nights later. Although Nicoll called *Remorse* worthy of comment, the reviews were "mixed," as well they might be.[14] The play lasted nearly five hours to which the

London *Times,* in a January twenty-fifth review, strenuously objected. The *Times* found the play's plot to be "'singularly involved
and laboured . . . ,'" lacking in versimilitude, and replete with
flat, declamatory characters.[15] A fresh look at *Remorse* will very
likely not yield a different judgment; but Coleridge did put a
great deal of time into the play, and there are some elements deserving of review, if only to make unnecessary any rereading of
the original.

In general, *Remorse* is *Osorio*[16] with different names for the cast
of characters and an extended scene here and there. Set in Spain
during the reign of Phillip II, the action takes place just at the close
of the civil wars against the Moors, and involves as one method of
creating dramatic tension the ramifications of the edict which
sentenced the Moors with death if apprehended wearing Moresco
apparel. The central conflict in the play is that between good and
evil manifest respectively in the characters of two brothers, Don
Alvar (the elder and the good) and Don Ordonio (the younger
and the evil). Coleridge intends that plot, action, and character
all move to realize the passion of remorse. To this end the Abel-
Cain motif proceeds. The play is much too involved in its plot
structure for more than superficial summary here. Briefly, Don
Alvar has years earlier been the victim of his brother's jealous
machinations and according to plan has been set upon by pirates
while off fighting for his father, Valdez. He has, however, managed to escape being killed by these assassins, whose leader was
the Moorish chieftain, Isidore, a man in the employ of the fell
Ordonio. When the play opens, Alvar, disguised as a Moresco
chieftain, has returned to Granada, his home, accompanied by his
faithful servant, Zulimez. He seeks not revenge but rather the
opportunity of bringing his brother to a state of remorse for what
he has tried to do. Alvar believes at this point that not only has
Ordonio tried to have him assassinated but also that Ordonio is
now married to Valdez' ward and his own former betrothed,
Donna Theresa.

Even at this point, sorting out who knows what is a major task
for the reader. Alvar knows that Ordonio has tried to have him
killed, but Ordonio does not know that the plot has failed. Valdez,
the father, and Theresa, his ward, believe with Ordonio that Alvar
has been killed although they, of course, do not know of Ordonio's
insidious part in the supposed tragedy. Alvar does not know that

Theresa is not married to Ordonio, but waits, faithful to his memory, hopeful that he might have escaped from the pirates. Ordonio, throughout these years, has, with his father's help, attempted to persuade her to marry him.

As for villainy, Ordonio is surely among the chief exponents of evil, but he is accompanied and even outdone by the bloodthirsty inquisitor, Monviedro, whose presence hangs ominously over both Moors and Spaniards. Monviedro is useful structurally in the play, for his inhuman treatment of the Moors in the name of Christianity gives Coleridge the opportunity to speak through the mouth of Alhadra, Moorish wife of Isidore, who in her harangue against this so-called Christianity reiterates the following point: that true Christianity is more than a series of dogma, that its ethical values are, or should be, universal, that under the Inquisition they have become distorted and perverted by those who are Christian in name only, as is Monviedro.

In Act II a meeting between Isidore and Ordonio, henchman and instigator, respectively, in the crime against Alvar, takes place. Once again Ordonio desires the services of Isidore. This time he wants the Moor to play the part of a sorcerer in order to convince Theresa that Alvar is indeed dead. In this way she will be free to marry Ordonio. At this point Isidore reveals that Alvar lives and that he himself wants no part in further plotting. He does, however, send Ordonio to a wizard's cottage. The wizard turns out to be Alvar, but his disguise is such that Ordonio fails to recognize him. Ordonio asks the disguised Alvar to help him in a plot to convince Theresa of his brother's death. Alvar agrees.

From here the play drags through three more acts to its obvious conclusion. Act III, scene i, contains the scene with the wizard and the entire cast gathered in Valdez' great hall. Here, in the midst of magic incantations, the wizard reveals to the entire company a picture of the plot to kill Alvar. Ordonio mutters, "Duped! duped! duped!"; Monviedro rushes on stage and takes the wizard prisoner. Valdez and Theresa mourn for the betrayed Alvar. In scene ii, Ordonio has settled on Isidore as the scapegoat and sets about plotting his death, while Valdez and Theresa hurry off to find Alvar's grave. Act IV, scene i, is involved with the murder of Isidore in a murky cave. This is one of the more memorable scenes, Gothic in impact, with the maw of the dank cavern ever present in the mind and vision of the audience. When Coleridge finally saw this scene played, he could not believe that he had created such a distillation of evil.[17]

The scene is illumined by torchlight. Isidore, lured to the cave by Ordonio, relates a morbid dream he has had. The substance of the dream follows: Isidore has earlier felt himself falling into a deep cavern, but before hitting bottom or being totally enveloped in Stygian blackness, he has awakened. In answer to the dream, Ordonio relates a story which tells of how he has lured a traitor into a murky cavern and killed him. Upon hearing this, Isidore casts off his cloak, draws his sword, and begins to fight with Ordonio. But Ordonio quickly disarms the Moor, flinging his sword far back into the cavern. As Isidore runs to retrieve it, Ordonio follows and pushes him over the brink into a deep chasm. He returns alone saying, "I have hurl'd him down the chasm! treason for treason./ He dreamt of it: henceforward let him sleep,/ A dreamless sleep, from which no wife can wake him./ His dream too is made out—Now for his friend." (IV. i. 168–71) Ordonio then exits in search of the wizard whom he believes to be in league with Isidore. These lines scarcely indicate in their callousness any capacity for regret. Throughout the play, Ordonio seems incapable of that compassion and empathy requisite to remorse, but regret must be effected and so the play continues. Act IV, scene ii, shifts to the dungeon where Theresa has gone, drawn by a desire to hear more from the ill-fated wizard to whom she feels inexplicably drawn. She believes nature never would have cloaked evil in a form so noble. In view of the wizard's magical talents, this is a somewhat unconvincing view for a wellborn maid to hold. Theresa is joined in the dungeon by Valdez, who again admonishes her to forget the wronged Alvar and marry Ordonio. The reader again must remember that Valdez and Theresa do not really know the extent of Ordonio's involvement in Alvar's supposed fate. Theresa, however, distrusts Ordonio intuitively. For this reason, she will have no part of her guardian's suggestion. Scene iii shifts dramatically to show Alhadra, the bereaved Moresco woman, revealing to the Moors the foul manner of her husband Isidore's murder. She is bent on vengeance and the audience rests assured that she will get it.

Act V attempts to knit all of these threads together and to bring about the climax of the play. Once again the scene shifts to the dungeon. Theresa enters. At this time Alvar reveals his true identity to her and finally, after many histrionics on her part, convinces her that he is indeed her beloved Alvar. At this point, Ordonio, bent on wiping out the wizard, enters bearing a goblet, "a libation to old Pluto," which contains a deadly poison. He offers it to Alvar who refuses it and dashes it to the ground. Here begin the most farfetched of a series of unlikely incidents. Alvar, instead of being killed instantly by Ordonio's sword, launches forth into a long harangue against Ordonio, in which he charges him with cowardice, infamy, and shallowness:

> Mountebank and villain!
> What then art thou? For shame, put up thy sword!
> What boots a weapon in a withered arm?
> I fix mine eye upon thee, and thou tremblest!
> I speak, and fear and wonder crush thy rage,
> And turn it to a motionless distraction!
> Thou blind self-worshipper! thy pride, thy cunning,
> Thy faith in universal villainy,
> Thy shallow sophisms, thy pretended scorn
> For all thy human brethren—out upon them!
> What have they done for thee? have they given thee peace?
> Cured thee of starting in thy sleep? or made
> The darkness pleasant when thou wak'st at midnight?
> Art happy when alone? Can'st walk by thyself
> With even step and quiet cheerfulness?
> Yet, yet thou may'st be saved—   (V. i. 151–66)

Nothing in Ordonio's character would indicate the temporary meekness with which he attends to these words. That he would stay and listen to Alvar's long diatribe is inconceivable. Equally inconceivable is the guilt he manifests after hearing the lines. Momentarily, he writhes in the throes of a guilty conscience; then, suddenly, he rushes at Alvar in an attempt to kill him. At this point Theresa intervenes saying, "Ordonio! 'tis thy brother!" (l. 195). At these words, Ordonio abruptly switches his intent from murder to suicide and attempts to fall upon his own sword! Naturally, Alvar and Theresa intervene and thwart him. He now asks forgiveness of Alvar and appears to show remorse over the murder of Isidore. Here Isidore's bereaved wife, Alhadra, and a company of Moors rush on stage. Ordonio makes his confession to Alhadra. She stabs him (at last a realistic action!), and then she and her company flee, as Ordonio in his atonement scene has wished. As the stage direction notes, Valdez then comes on stage and ". . . rushes into Alvar's arms." Theresa and Alvar receive his blessing, while Ordonio, son, brother, lover, lies on the cold floor adjacent to this happy scene! Alvar's summation is a pronouncement upon the efficacy of conscience and the metamorphosis which conscience undergoes when the small voice is heard:

> Delights so full, if unalloyed with grief,
> Were ominous. In these strange dread events
> Just heaven instructs us with an awful voice,
> That Conscience rules us e'en against our choice.
> Our inward Monitress to guide or warn,
> If listened to; but if repelled with scorn,
> At length as dire Remorse, she reappears,
> Works in our guilty hopes, and selfish fears!
> Still bids, Remember! and still cries, Too late!
> And while she scares us, goads us to our fate.
>   (V. i. 285–94)

That Coleridge was in deadly earnest when he wrote *Remorse* is, perhaps unfortunately, all too true. He was himself affected by the play, as the letter to John Rickman illustrates. Another letter in praise of *Remorse* was directed to Robert Southey in 1813.[18] In this letter, Coleridge names as the two best qualities in the play ". . . the simplicity and Unity of the Plot" and the play's "metrics." He defends also the charge levied against the play that it wanted pathos. He states, "As to the outcry that the Remorse is not pathetic (meaning such pathos as convulses us in Isabella or the Gamester) the answer is easy—True! the Poet never meant that it should be. It is as pathetic as the Hamlet, or the Julius Caesar." [19] Regrettably, Coleridge is not seeing himself as others see him. For the modern reader, the play's plot is both confused and lacking in focus; as for the "metrics," there is not that variety which characterizes the Shakespearean play. In no way is *Remorse* comparable to either *Hamlet* or *Julius Caesar*. This is surely a classic case of wishful thinking on Coleridge's part. Even when the play is compared with one of its own kind, it suffers. Byron's *Manfred,* never a poetic drama to receive accolades, is nonetheless infinitely superior to *Remorse*. Though one tires in the former of the egomania of Count Manfred, of the histrionics manifest in

his struggle with the Chamois Hunter, of his rant against mankind, of his impossibly idealistic devotion to Astarte, still one can
feel the impact of the characterization, delight in much of the
poetry, rise at moments to a sense of grandeur which intermittently comes through in the drama, and remember at the end that
the play realizes a unity of intent and accomplishment. Byron's
own comment on *Remorse*, if it were serious (and it likely was
not), provides a sorry general commentary on the state of the
drama at that time. In a letter to Coleridge, dated March 31, 1815,
Byron wrote as follows: "We have had nothing to mention in the
same breath as Remorse for very many years." [20] One might remember *Manfred* with mild affection, but *Remorse* with regret
only.

After looking at *Remorse*, there is no need for a summary of
Coleridge's next play, *Zapolya*.[21] It was offered, as was *Remorse*,
to Drury Lane for production; unlike *Remorse*, it was rejected.
Zapolya, as the advertisement states, was written ". . . in humble
imitation of the *Winter's Tale* of Shakespeare." [22] Coleridge
had high hopes for the play, and he wished it to be considered
"a Christmas tale." [23] A letter to John May, written on September 27, 1815, indicates his desire to see the play produced: "I
am now compleating a Tragedy for Drury Lane, which I trust will
better deserve success than the Remorse, though I shall be more
than content if it should meet with the same." [24]

III Zapolya

Zapolya, like *Remorse*, has a foreign land for its setting. Here
the land is Illyria. The play proceeds in two parts, composed of
Part I, the prelude, and Part II, acts I–IV. The names of the characters demonstrate, as does the setting, the Romantic interest in
the strange and remote. Queen Zapolya, as the play opens, is
about to be widowed and left with an infant son, as traitors plot
to usurp the throne. Loyal to her is Raab Kiuprili, Illyrian chieftain. Loyal also is Ragozzi, father of Glycine, who is at the time
the play gets under way a lovely maiden given over to the care of
Casimir and his good wife, Lady Sarolta. Disloyal to Zapolya is
Casimir, Raab's son, now allied with the villain of the piece,
Emerick, whose struggle for power has brought all of this about.
Between the close of the Prelude and the beginning of Act I, some
twenty years elapse. Undoubtedly, this created a major obstacle

in considering the play for production. Very briefly, the plot is as follows: after twenty years, the anonymous heir, Prince Andreas the son of Zapolya, is found to be in the care of an old mountaineer, Bathrick. It seems that the loyal Ragozzi has deposited the child with Bathrick at the time when Zapolya and he were fleeing for their lives. Raab Kiuprili has been hiding out in a forest with Queen Zapolya. During this twenty-year period, the kingdom has been ruled by Emerick and his supporter Casimir. Ultimately, however, the true heir to the throne, Andrea, discovers his mother in the wood and, with the help of Raab, defeats the false Emerick and his forces and wins the hand of Glycine, ward of Kiuprili's son, the traitor Casimir. Casimir repents of his part in the treacherous plot, and he and his lady, the good Sarolta, are given sanctuary under the rightful government of Prince Andreas. On the whole, the plot is a trite one, fit for melodrama but most assuredly not fit for tragedy. Coleridge, however, was understandably hurt when he learned that the critics had received the play with derision.[25]

The freedom theme, an evil tyrant having gained the upper hand and being finally overcome by justice or goodness, is fairly common to Coleridge's dramas, as it was to much of his early poetry. In summary, all of the plays are, for the most part, written in blank verse; all contain elements of both the baroque and the gothic; all deal in some fashion with men who should have been great, but whose passions outstripped their reason; all are shot through with underdeveloped characters and characterized by declamatory dialogue and rhetoric which pays little, if any, attention to achieving any degree of verisimilitude. After reading these "poetic dramas," no one would wonder that they did not meet with more favorable reception, but many might wonder why a man of Coleridge's talents would have spent so much time and energy in the production of such trivial matter.

CHAPTER 8

The Prose: Part I, Literary Criticism

THE prose of Samuel Taylor Coleridge is prodigious in both amount and scope. Its range of subject demands of the reader that he be a philosopher, a theologian, a literary critic, a political scientist, a logician, a metaphysician, an epistolarian, a historian, and so on. This staggering number of roles is, however, but one of the complications facing any student of the prose. In addition are the following obstacles: the fragmentary nature of many of the manuscripts; the unavailability of much of the material; the demands made upon the reader's knowledge of both ancient and foreign languages. Further than these external complications are those occurring in both direction and organization. For example, in the lecture notes pertaining to the literary criticism, Coleridge might well indicate that he was going to do one thing at some future date, and then when that date arrived proceed to do something entirely different. In one such instance, an announced lecture on *Romeo and Juliet* emerged a week later in lecture as a diatribe against the critics of flogging in British public schools. Another illustration of this organizational problem occurs in Chapter XIII, Volume I, of the *Biographia*. Here Coleridge is in the midst of explaining his principle of the reconciliation of opposites and his concept of imagination. The reader has every reason and right to expect a complete explanation, only to be frustrated by having Coleridge announce that a letter from an unnamed friend has dissuaded him from discussing the concepts further at this time. The upshot is that these concepts are never fully explicated. In view of these complications and organizational problems, the adjectives "labyrinthian" and "circumlocutory" are appropriate to any general description of the prose. Nonetheless, to dismiss the prose as "muddled," "peripheral," "obscure," "unsystematic," and the like, is not only to beg the question, but also to miss at least one-half and perhaps three-fourths of the essential Coleridge.

That which illumines the man and his work can be found perhaps more accurately in the prose than in the poetry, although one must have the endurance requisite to such an undertaking. In truth, studies in recent years have attended more and more to the prose and, conversely, less and less to the poetry. Two full-length studies of the literary criticism by Richards[1] and Fogle[2] are now available, as is the Muirhead study of Coleridge as philosopher, and perhaps most exhaustive of all, Professor Coburn's fine edition, only partially completed at this time, of Coleridge's note-books.[3] No overview of the prose is available at present, nor is there likely to be one for some time to come. As Bate remarks, "Closely as some of his works have been examined, his prose writings as a whole still constitute one of the most challenging unexplored territories in the history of critical thinking." [4]

In this present study of Coleridge's prose, his literary criticism and his philosophical and religious essays are important in that order. The impossibility of covering all of any one of these important areas within the scope of this study is obvious. For this reason, attention will be centered upon two major tenets of the theoretical criticism and primarily upon Coleridge's practical criticism as it applies to Wordsworth and Shakespeare. A cursory glance at the philosophy as it relates to the criticism will be found in the ensuing chapter.

I *Literary Criticism: Theory and Principles*

Coleridge stands as the theoretical critic between Dryden (who was only passingly so) and, in modern times, I. A. Richards (though he might deny it). The Neo-classicists of the eighteenth century were certainly not interested in abstruse criticism but, rather, were dedicated to Aristotelian analysis, which they hailed as "common-sense" criticism. For them, theories of "aesthetics" were capricious, fanciful, and neither to be trusted nor indulged. They were, for the most part, interested in seeing whether or not a work of art or a poem measured up to Nature, its model. To them, the purpose and goal of art was to imitate that perfection of order seen in Nature. The Victorians, on the other hand, were for the most part happy to leave esthetics and theory (though the notable exceptions of Pater and Wilde contradict this) and devote themselves to seeing the object as it really was in itself, looking at works of art for purposes of moral instruction, or making historical studies of literature. They were not only distrustful of Coleridge's theory of criticism, which they termed his wilful "obscurity," but were also repelled by it.[5]

As has been indicated in the preceding discussion of his poetry, dichotomies and antithetical constructs had great appeal for Coleridge. When he said that every man was born either an Aristotelian or a Platonist,[6] he may well have paved the way for the famous critical distinctions which were to mark literary criticism from the nineteenth century to the present day. In support of this, Professor Huntington Cairns traces two major aspects exhibited by criticism from its beginnings. The one involves the analysis of literature; the other involves the explanation of literature. This second, Cairns states, seeks not to judge but rather to explain, in order that the reader may derive greater pleasure from his consequent greater understanding of the work. This second aspect, which criticism has exhibited, attempts to see the work as a whole, or at least attempts to see *wholly* an adequate segment of the work,[7] and it is to this aspect that Coleridge's critical point of view attends. Whenever critics talk about the work as a "whole" or about seeing the work "wholly," one can expect to find the label, "organic" appended; and it was Coleridge who was instrumental in developing this concept.

In placing Coleridge as critic within his proper frame of reference, that is, within the Romantic mode of criticism, Bate's discussion of the differences between Romantic and Neo-classic criticism is helpful. For the Neo-classic, as has been indicated in Chapter II, art must copy life; thus the closer art comes to making a faithful copy of Nature, its order and universality, the closer art comes to a correspondence with truth. For this reason, art should seek to be objective; it must be so if it is to turn itself outward in order to reflect accurately the grand order in the universe. The unique, the rare, the bizarre are beyond the concern of the artist because they are not "universal" but single, often accidental. The Neo-classicists, believing this to be true, rejected any artistic concern for such single or unique characteristics, confident that the universe was not composed of freaks and exceptions, but rather of ordered patterns recurring with regularity and reliability which, when reflected by man in art and literature, were evidence of the operation of reason and common sense. The Romantic poet and critic was, on the other hand, far more interested in a manifestation of the individual, that is, in what makes each man and each work uniquely himself and itself. Thus the Romantics often chafed under the strictures of eighteenth-century neo-classical "rules" and cast about for that vitalistic approach to art and to life which held meaning for each individual artist and man.[8] This is not to say that Coleridge was not interested in "universals," for as a theoretical critic, his interest in such follows by definition. In order to illustrate these universals, or principles, Coleridge often utilized the bizarre, the strange, and the particular. For example, he used a skeletal, bright-eyed mariner and a lady from a "far countree" as agents to effect his central theme, the power and efficacy of love. From a neo-classical point of view, these would be strange creatures indeed to select in order to effect such a universal theme.

In addressing himself to the matter of Coleridge's theoretical criticism, the student is handicapped once again, for it is only too true, as Watson contends, that no critic of today seems to be able to agree with any other on what Coleridge, in his role of critic, actually thought or said. All modern critics seem to agree, however, that Coleridge as critic is of first importance.[9] In general this dilemma is best resolved by going directly to those primary sources which have to do not only with principles of criticism as Coleridge conceived them, but also with the practical criticism which appears to be consistent with them.

The chief source of the criticism, one that has been culled again and again, is the *Biographia Literaria*. As its foremost editor, Shawcross has stated the purpose of this work lay in ". . . the desire, on Coleridge's part, to state clearly, and defend adequately, his own poetic creed." [10] Although the *Biographia* is crammed with material irrelevant to the above purpose, this theme and its substance recur throughout the two volumes. Perhaps one explanation for this irrelevant mass is that not only was the *Biographia* supposedly written in one year, but also it underwent a number of publication problems between 1816 and 1817 which both contributed to, and resulted from, Coleridge's ill health and mental anguish.[11] Probably the reception accorded the work did not help his spirits either, for neither the general public nor his friend, Wordsworth, was pleased with the work.[12] Most certainly the work combined all of the problems indigenous to Coleridge's prose, but it is vital nonetheless to a study of his criticism.

. . .

Coleridge's first critical principle or tenet is the theory of "organic unity." When applied to a work of art, a poem, it means simply that the parts of the poem, as the parts of a plant, have an organic relationship to each other. A "legitimate" poem is to Coleridge one in which the parts support and explain each other. It should be made clear that they do so not in any mechanical sense, which would lend itself wholly to objective analysis, but rather in a dynamic sense which enables them to interrelate accordingly. The poem is analogous to a plant and not to a machine; it is therefore a living organism which has life independent of its creator's continuing surveillance, although never wholly independent, as would be an entity in a vacuum. This latter distinction is important. The poem has grown out of a multitude of concepts, matter, things. These are all essential to it, for the poem is a synthesis of them all. In the sense that the plant lives, having taken life from earth, air, sky, and water, so similarly the poem lives, having taken life from its creator, from history, from universal experience. To truncate it from its essentials would be to kill it. In this respect, Coleridge is not truly an ancestor of the "new" critics, for, as Fogle points out, he would never have agreed to the total divorce of the work of art from the mind of its creator.[13] Coleridge is essentially a Platonist striving to realize the One in the Many by pushing ever outward to a greater synthesis beyond the work in question, yet recognizing the complexity and essentiality of all that has gone into its creation. Fogle has cautioned against the equating of the poem with a tree, or some other botanical species; he has pointed out, and rightly, that the analogy is metaphorical and as such stands not only for implied likeness, but also for implied difference.[14] At the risk of oversimplifying the problem, the chemical equation which takes hydrogen and oxygen in specified combination to get water may well demonstrate that the parts of a poem only in the *right* combination compose the dynamic work of art, the new product. What Fogle admonishes the reader to remember is that the artist has a vitally essential part in the creation of the work of art, that art does not just "happen," but that it is created. This creative process, its components and proper combinations, constitutes one of the major interests of Samuel Taylor Coleridge.

The second tenet in Coleridge's critical theory is the principle or theory of "the reconciliation of opposites," which is allied closely with the tenet of "organic unity." Coleridge held that two opposite, but equal, forces will react to, and interact upon, one another to the end that a third force or element will result, which is different from the sum of both, or from either one taken singly. This general principle can be applied to almost anything in art or life. As Baker points out in his study, *The Sacred River,* the theory can extend to specifics; for example, the two halves of a metaphor (tenor and vehicle), put together and reconciled, make up the whole metaphor and its total effectiveness.[15] Or the theory can extend to "universals"; for example, mind and heart must work together within the artist or poet to produce a work of high imagination. Or, in a consideration of the nature of Nature, man must both perceive and create in order to *conceive* of Nature wholly. "Dejection: An Ode" serves as a specific illustration, of course, of this utilization. The theory may be extended to encompass antithetical pairs which, when applied to literature or life by the poet, illuminate what has initially been obscure. The constructs of imagination and fancy, reason and understanding, serve as examples of these pairs.[16] Further than these usages, the principle may be evoked in an attempt to reconcile the universal with the particular. The extremes of eighteenth-century criticism (emphasis upon universals) might be reconciled with the extremes of nineteenth-century criticism (emphasis upon particulars). Coleridge himself alluded to this reconciliation as a possibility when he commented that the French school of criticism set against the Johnsonian school of criticism must be reconciled in a third which would be neither the one nor the other, but something lying between the two. In a philosophical way, the theory can be utilized to define reality as something that lies neither totally without man nor totally within; that is, neither in the object nor in the subject, but somewhere in a third or middle ground, a combination of the two, yet more than the sum of the one plus the other.

The two critical tenets discussed operate throughout Coleridge's critical theory. In practice, as seen in the chapters on the poetry, Coleridge used them often. They are probably his chief contribution to modern criticism. Another, more minor, of his contributions is the following: an emphasis upon pleasure as the purpose of poetry serves as a contribution to esthetic critical theory. For Coleridge the immediate object of a poem is the communication of pleasure. In this respect poetry differs from science: "A poem is that species of composition, which is opposed to works of science, by proposing for its *immediate* object pleasure, not truth; and from all other species (having *this* object in common with it) it is discriminated by proposing to itself such delight from the *whole*, as is compatible with a distinct gratification from each component *part*." [17]

Not only does this comment ally Coleridge with the first critical tenet, that of organic unity, but also it allies him firmly with the second aspect of criticism as discussed by Professor Cairns. It sets Coleridge's critical theory against that of the Neo-classicists who were more avowedly interested in poetry as a reflection of truth in imitation of life than in poetry as an experience in pleasure. In further support of this point are Coleridge's own words concerning the reader and critic: "The reader should be carried forward, not merely or chiefly by the mechanical impulse of curiosity, or by a restless desire to arrive at the final solution; but by the pleasurable activity of mind excited by the attractions of the journey itself." [18] As Watson contends, Coleridge was not primarily interested in judging a work as good or bad, but rather in reflecting upon it, explaining it, and deriving pleasure from this consequent better understanding of it.[19]

Coleridge's central interest as a critic, however, is not in the effect of the poem on the reader, but rather in the process by which a poem is conceived. Modern critics hold Coleridge to be one of the foremost exponents of the *method* of criticism.[20] Inextricably involved in Coleridge's dedication to the study of, and attempt to explain, the creative process are the two terms *Imagination* and *Fancy*. These terms occur again and again in his criticism and for this reason demand explanation. Unfortunately, Coleridge himself never fully explicated these terms, although he did define them.[21] Coleridge separated the functions of the first term into two categories: primary and secondary. Professor Richard Fogle, in his lucid study of Coleridge's criticism, has this to say: "Coleridge distinguishes between the primary imagination common to all, which is the instrument of his psychology and philosophy, and the secondary or specifically poetic imagination, which is the instrument of his criticism." [22] In Coleridge's own words, he holds the primary imagination to be "the living Power and prime Agent of all human Perception, and as a repetition in the finite mind of the eternal act of creation in the infinite I AM." [23] The secondary imagination is an "echo" of the primary and as such it differs not in kind but in degree and in "the mode of its operation." The secondary imagination operates in one of two ways: "It dissolves, diffuses, dissipates, in order to recreate; or where this process is rendered impossible, yet still at all events its struggles to idealize and to unify." [24] Coleridge calls this force "vital" and places it in opposition to *objects* which are "essentially fixed and dead." [25] Objects are of course the concern of *Fancy*, and earlier in the *Biographia* Coleridge has noted the distinction between imagination and fancy. Later on in the work, he has defined fancy as ". . . no other than a mode of Memory emancipated from the order of time and space." [26] The fancy plays merely with "fixities and definites." It receives from association, but it never creates. The use which Coleridge makes of the construct, Imagination and Fancy, is considerable, and an understanding of it is essential to any study of his critical theory.

In addition to a consideration of primary imagination, the student of Coleridge's theoretical criticism needs to direct his attention to the secondary, or "poetic," imagination. Chapter thirteen, volume two, of the *Biographia* is initially significant. Here Coleridge states that the creative act is active in man as God is active in the world. Consequently, the poet brings to his subject or matter such vital energy and dynamic power that the dry materials become imbued with life to the end that the work becomes "organic." [27] The poem so conceived is one with beauty. It is the secondary imagination which supplies this vital energy requisite to creation. At one point Coleridge chose to designate this specifically creative force "Esemplastic," meaning to shape into one.[28] He wished to disabuse his readers of the concept of imagination held by eighteenth-century writers, where the term was often equated with fancy. Coleridge stressed the fact that imagination was a great deal more than an "aggregative and associative power." Indeed, at one point he chastised Wordsworth for confusing this aggregative and associative function of fancy with the creative power of imagination.

Unfortunately, there is no single way to clarify for all readers for all time the distinction between the secondary imagination and the fancy. Put simply, the function of fancy is one of ordering and classifying past experience which has been stored in the memory. The fancy cannot *change* objects or remembered experience; it can merely rearrange objects or recall experience. The secondary imagination can change (by dissolving and diffusing) objects, or it can *create* objects a priori. An illustration of this lies in Coleridge's contention that the nurse in *Romeo and Juliet* is not simply a composite picture of all the nurses Shakespeare has known, but rather that she is that plus Shakespeare's own imaginative power to "individuate," that is to bring to the nurse something which makes her uniquely Shakespeare's creation.[29] Certainly, as seen here, the imagination can and does utilize the function of fancy, but it is the imagination alone which creates the great poem. The way in which the poems of high imagination rise above the juvenilia and certain of the minor poems is a marked illustration of the difference between the two functions.

To keep all of these definitions and distinctions in mind is rather a chore. Coleridge often used the terms for classification, and his usage may help to clarify the terms themselves. For example, for Coleridge, Milton typified a poet of imagination; Cowley, one of fancy.[30] Chaucer and Shakespeare had highly imaginative minds,[31] while Wordsworth, on occasion, resorted to fancy, though on the whole his mind too was imaginative.

There were other characteristics to look for in a poem, however. First of all, a great poem can be identified as one to which the reader is compelled to return again and again.[32] A great poem is one in which no word may be altered without resultant loss to the poem as a "legitimate" work of art.[33] Another quality to be sought in a poem is the combination of natural thought with natural diction. These result from the combination within the poet of heart with head, or as Coleridge puts it, the reconciliation of heart with head.[34] This quality derives, of course, from an implementation in the creative process of the second tenet, the reconciliation of opposites. Coleridge points to two older poets, Donne and Cowley, as examples of those who sacrificed heart to head. He finds most of his contemporaries, however, to be even less acceptable, for they have tended to sacrifice, ". . . both heart and head to point and drapery," that is, to ". . . the glare and glitter of a perpetual, yet broken and heterogeneous imagery, or rather to an amphibious something, made up, half of image, and half of abstract meaning."[35] Still, as has been observed, Coleridge was not so much interested in disparaging a work as in enjoying it. For him the critic's main task should ever be to point out the beauties in a work rather than the defects.[36]

II *Literary Criticism: Application*
Wordsworth and Shakespeare

It has been remarked that Coleridge's greatest work was Wordsworth.[37] Although this comment is undoubtedly facetious, Coleridge's comments on Wordsworth's poetry and on the *Lyrical Ballads* per se serve to demonstrate the application of his own theory of criticism. Coleridge undoubtedly had more to say about Wordsworth than he did about any other of his contemporaries. And the reason for this was that Coleridge admired Wordsworth enormously, classifying him just under Milton and Shakespeare in the galaxy of great poets. For Coleridge, the belief that Wordsworth was an "original poetic genius" struck him in his twenty-fourth year and prompted him to look into the reasons for this.[38] Out of this investigation grew the now famous distinction between imagination and fancy previously discussed. Coleridge attributed Wordsworth's peculiar genius to his essential quality of combining ". . . deep feeling with profound thought." [39] In Wordsworth's great poems, Coleridge saw imagination operating at its highest.

The reconciliation of heart with head, he thought, was effected in such a poem as "Tintern Abbey," a poem of high imagination. But Coleridge was, for all his faults, too much the critic to miss the fact that such poems as "The Thorn" and "Simon Lee" were not in the same class with "Tintern Abbey." He saw the former as among the humblest and least elevating of all the poems.[40] Coleridge retrospectively criticized the *Lyrical Ballads* by discriminating among these poems, and he did so on most counts fairly and accurately. Indeed his chief criticism of Wordsworth centers not upon the poems per se, but rather upon Wordsworth's 1800 *Preface*, which was written as a kind of apologia for the poems. There is some justification for believing that Coleridge was in part criticizing himself, for Coleridge was certainly as involved in the theory which gave rise to the poems as was Wordsworth himself. Still there is no doubt but that Wordsworth was chiefly responsible for the 1800 *Preface*.[41] In Coleridge's opinion, Wordsworth's attempt to justify the inclusion of certain poems irritated people

more than the poems themselves did. Coleridge felt that a deletion of one hundred lines of poetry would have avoided approximately nine-tenths of the criticism which redounded upon them,
and that such a deletion would have strengthened the poets' posi-
tions considerably.[42] In addition, it seemed to Coleridge most unfortunate that Wordsworth attempted in the *Preface* to advance a
comprehensive theory of poetry which would extend to all poetry,
when the specific poems incorporated into the *Lyrical Ballads* had
been written avowedly in the nature of an experiment.

In support of this point of view, Coleridge discussed the different approaches taken by the two poets. He stated that he did not
remember which of them had proposed the plan for the *Lyrical
Ballads*, but that both of them had agreed to write a series of
poems, each of which would fall into one of two categories: those
poems that were concerned with the supernatural supernatural
and those that were concerned with the natural supernatural.
Coleridge was to direct his attention to the former, that is, to
". . . persons and characters supernatural, or at least romantic;
yet so as to transfer from our inward nature a human interest and
a semblance of truth sufficient to procure for these shadows of
imagination that willing suspension of disbelief for the moment,
which constitutes poetic faith." [43] Wordsworth, on the other hand,
was to address himself to the natural supernatural, and thereby to
seek in the familiar scenes and faces around him a wonder and a
loveliness indicative of higher truths.[44] Out of these two approaches, Coleridge produced dark ladies, glittering-eyed mariners, strange Lewtis, and lovely Christabels, while Wordsworth
saw in the meanest flower that blows, in the ruins of an old abbey,
in idiot boys and little girls, indications of eternal truths which lay
"too deep for tears." The well-known statement of Coleridge's that
Wordsworth was to ". . . consider the influences of fancy and imagination as they are manifested in poetry," whereas he himself
was to ". . . investigate the seminal principle" gives some indica-
tion again of the crucial difference in their two approaches.[45] As
usual Coleridge has a far more complex and philosophically deep-
seated approach in mind. For example, he speaks of Wordsworth
as dealing with the "poetic fruitage" of the tree, that which is seen
more easily, whereas he states that he himself is concerned with
the "trunk" and "roots" of the tree, that is, with its generative be-

ginning, its source of vitality.[46] Although the product may be Wordsworth's, the process of production is the concern of Coleridge.

Nonetheless, it undoubtedly seemed to Coleridge that the poems in the *Lyrical Ballads* ought to be allowed to stand or fall on the basis of individual merit rather than receive shoddy support from an after-the-fact preface. Further than this objection, however, he had other and more specific quarrels with this preface. For example, he objected to Wordsworth's statement that the poems were purposely expressed in ". . . language really used by men . . . (purified indeed from what appear to be its real defects from all lasting and rational causes of dislike or disgust)." [47] The speciousness of this claim was too much for Coleridge on two counts: first of all, he believed a poem should attempt to approximate the "ideal" rather than the "real"—that is, it ought to emulate what ought to be rather than what is; secondly, there was no "lingua communis," for language not only varied from country to country, but also from county to county. The peasant was not a peasant universal, as Wordsworth contended, but rather a poor facsimile thereof.[48]

In Chapter twenty of the *Biographia*, Coleridge advanced what has now become an established point of view, namely that there were two Wordsworths: the one, author of the Lucy poems, of "We Are Seven," "Expostulation and Reply," "The Tables Turned," and the like; the other, author of "Tintern Abbey," "Resolution and Independence," and the like. The latter poems, though perhaps not as immediately recognizable as Wordsworth's, were nonetheless much more to Coleridge's liking and, in his opinion, deserving of much more acclamation. In these poems, the diction is not assimilated rustic, but elevated and magnificently appropriate to the themes.[49] These poems were, in Coleridge's judgment, fine, inspired, contemplative, imaginative, and therefore inspirational to the reader. Most contemporary critics would agree with Coleridge's evaluation. It was Coleridge's hope that the poems in this second category would become more prevalent as time passed.[50]

The next section of the *Biographia* to be devoted to Wordsworth takes up the whole of Chapter twenty-two, volume two. In this famous chapter, Coleridge lists the defects and the excellencies of Wordsworth's poetry, taking care always to reiterate that the excellencies far outweigh the defects. In actuality, however, he lists five defects and discusses them for some eighteen pages, while he lists six excellencies and devotes but fourteen pages to their discussion. In brief, the defects are: an inconstancy of style; a "matter-of-factness" which characterizes certain poems and tends to reduce the concern to the "accidental" rather than to the universal; "an undue predilection for the *dramatic* form in certain poems"; "occasional prolixity, repetition, and an eddying, instead of progression, of thought"; and lastly, "thoughts and images too great for the subject." [51] The excellencies are: "an austere purity of language"; "a correspondent weight and sanity of the Thoughts and Sentiments won—not from books, but—from the poet's own meditative observation"; "the sinewy strength and originality of single lines and paragraphs"; "the perfect truth of nature in his images and descriptions"; "a union of deep and subtle thought with sensibility"; and finally "the gift of IMAGINATION in the highest and strictest sense of the word." [52] At a glance, many of the excellencies seem to contradict by their coincidence the defects. Coleridge does substantiate his points, however, by referring specifically to the text of the poems, and he does qualify wherever necessary by adding the phrase "in certain poems" to almost all enumerations.

The most astute observations are among those listed under *defects*, particularly the comments made on inconstancy of style and on matter-of-factness. Among the list of *excellencies*, most important is the recognition of Wordsworth's imaginative power, a power which entitles him to stand in the first rank of English poets.[53]

So much for Coleridge's practical criticism of Wordsworth. Now what of its consistency with Coleridge's theory of criticism? As Fogle has noted, the tenor of Coleridge's comments on Wordsworth's poetry appears on the surface to be neo-classic. The judicial aspect of dividing the characteristics into *defects* and *excellencies* makes the criticism appear this way. Such an approach is all too reminiscent of that taken by Dr. Johnson. Nonetheless, as Coleridge was perfectly aware, the ideal Wordsworth was a man of genius, potentially the greatest philosophical poet in the world; and if Wordsworth erred it was only in his occasional failure to obliterate the accidental from his poems. Coleridge, after all, saw Wordsworth as being in a state of growth; and he saw his poetry similarly. His overview of Wordsworth, therefore, was consistently *organic* (just as Wordsworth's development was organic) in spite of the judicial overtones of Coleridge's practical criticism of Wordsworth.[54]

The next substantial body of Coleridge's literary criticism is not found, for the most part, in the *Biographia,* but must be culled from marginalia, lecture notes, and from sections of *The Friend.*[55] These works are, of course, only a few of the many sources of the criticism. Until 1930, the literary criticism was available in part in an edition compiled by Mrs. Ernest Hartley Coleridge entitled *Literary Remains.* In 1930, however, Thomas Raysor brought out an admirable edition of Coleridge's Shakespearean criticism which superseded the other collection and made this material more readily available.[56]

Coleridge's Shakespearean criticism was distinguished for its "new look" at the Bard. On the whole, Coleridge provided an entirely different approach to Shakespeare from that taken by the great critics of the Neo-classic age. Chief among these was Dr. Samuel Johnson, who summarized and broadened the conservative, critical approach to Shakespeare in his *Preface to Shakespeare.*[57] In this preface, Johnson saw Shakespeare as one who mirrored the universal and general in nature, and who, though certainly aware of its existence, most assiduously avoided the accidental and particular as suitable thematic material. For Johnson, Shakespeare epitomized the poet of nature; the Bard's interest was seen to be centered in the general man rather than on any particular man. Shakespeare could thus be said to have no heroes, but rather to have characters one might expect to meet in everyday life.[58] Johnson saw this universality of character portrayal as one of the predominant "beauties" of Shakespeare's work. And indeed, like most Neo-classical critics, Johnson had divided Shakespeare's work into those characteristic categories of eighteenth-century criticism: beauties and defects. One of the chief among the latter was Shakespeare's habit of violating the unity of the drama. In particular, it seemed to Johnson, the poet violated the "unities of time and place."[59] Johnson believed, however, that these defects could and should be written out of the texts by contemporary emendation of the plays.[60] Johnson saw another "defect" in the dialogue which he found to be full of excessive rhetoric, circumlocutions, pompous diction,[61] and an excess of incident.[62] The reason which gave rise to these defects lay in the times themselves; Shakespeare was one writing for a horde of barbarians in an equally barbaric age.[63]

Such commentary is sufficient to indicate both Johnson's direction and tone. Although somewhat apologetic for Shakespeare's defects, Johnson concluded that Shakespeare was great in spite of them. In a sense, he looked upon Shakespeare paradoxically. The Bard was the natural man of genius, and as such he could not help but be great. Yet, the poet was so close to nature that he could not avoid inheriting some of the "exceptions" in nature. For this reason, Shakespeare reflected a certain lack of discipline, and discipline was a quality which the eighteenth-century man insisted on maintaining.

Samuel Taylor Coleridge's criticism of Shakespeare stands, in many respects, diametrically opposed to that of Johnson and, therefore, anticipates Romantic criticism of the nineteenth century. For Coleridge, Shakespeare is not only the natural man of genius, but also the poet of high imagination. Coleridge never apologizes for Shakespeare; he reveres him almost utterly. Coleridge's criticism is not an analysis per se, although it does contain analyses of parts of plays. Coleridge's Shakespearean criticism is in a larger sense interpretive and appreciative. This is to be expected, for such an approach is consistent with Coleridge's theory of criticism. For Coleridge, as later for Keats, Shakespeare is the Man of Achievement. His greatness lies in his ability to imbue his highly imaginative characters with blood, bone, and remarkable potentiality. Each of his characters is distinctly individual, and at the same time each reflects that which is universal in man. Shakespeare's art and talent are the chief concerns of Coleridge's criticism. Again, his purpose is to point up "beauties" rather than "defects." Because of this approach, Coleridge stands as the herald of that Romantic mode of criticism which prevailed in the nineteenth century and has extended well into the twentieth.[64] The Romantics were, of course, deeply interested in great personalities. This characteristic was not indigenous solely to English men of letters, but also marked German criticism and *belles-lettres*. That Coleridge was influenced by German writers with respect to critical theory and philosophy is well-known. The extent of this influence is, of course, beyond the scope of this study.[65]

Coleridge's concern with Shakespeare as a delineator of character identifies him as a critic more interested in the "literary" than in the "dramatic" talents of the Bard. In the twentieth century, such interest is viewed retrospectively as psychological. Certainly, Coleridge's commentary on the character of Hamlet gave rise to many of today's psychological interpretations. In initiating his commentary on *Hamlet*, Coleridge turned immediately to the character of Hamlet, as follows: "*Hamlet* was the play, or rather Hamlet himself was the character in the intuition and exposition of which I first made my turn for philosophical criticism, and especially for insight into the genius of Shakespeare, *noticed*." [66] For Coleridge, Hamlet was the man whose excessive reflection and contemplative habit served to militate against his taking action and to lead ultimately to the destruction not only of himself, but also of Polonius, Ophelia, and the King and Queen. Within this view, Hamlet is seen to be predominantly the ratiocinative meditator, the idealist personified. Coleridge calls him the "over-meditative Hamlet" and asserts that the final action of the play hinges upon "accidents." [67] The chief problem which confronts Hamlet is his own nature. He is a man fraught with a fundamental imbalance of thought and action. He is unable to reconcile these opposites in his nature. There is no counterpart within him to the contemplative, and this is the lack which precipitates the tragedy. [68] In Coleridge's own words: "In Hamlet I conceive him to have wished to exemplify the moral necessity of a due balance between our attention to outward objects and our meditation on inward thoughts— a due balance between the real and imaginary world. In Hamlet this balance does not exist. . . . Hence great, enormous, intellectual activity, and a consequent proportionate aversion to real action, with all its symptoms and accompanying qualities." [69] And later, following the famous soliloquy, "O that this too, too solid flesh would melt," Coleridge attributes this *tedium vitae* described above to: "The exhaustion of bodily feeling from perpetual exertion of mind." [70] Such remarks are undoubtedly a prelude to the later view of Hamlet as the introspective, overly contemplative, dreamer.

It is interesting to note Coleridge's observation that Hamlet's habit of mind runs continually to abstraction. He runs away from ". . . the particular in [to] the general. This aversion to personal, individual concerns, and escape to generalizations and general reasonings, is a most important characteristic." [71] Many are the critics who have claimed that Coleridge's own mind runs in similar fashion. Certainly the Hamlet criticism is convincingly presented, and one wonders if Coleridge's own propensity for abstraction may not have provided greater insight into the character of Hamlet, the Dane. It should be stressed, however, that *meditative* must not be equated with *indecisive*. To Coleridge, Hamlet was not indecisive: ". . . he knows well what he ought to do, and over and over, again he makes up his mind to do it."[72] It is simply that Hamlet's world is one of profound meditation and not one of action. He retires continually from the workaday world into that more real world which exists within himself.[73]

Although the general approach to the *Hamlet* criticism may be largely interpretive and, in that sense, "psychological," the general structure, as indicated in the sketchy notes, is descriptive. Coleridge takes up significant points in logical sequence, beginning with the appearance of the ghost on the ramparts and ending with a discussion of Act V, scenes i–ii. At this point, the discussion breaks into the foregoing commentary on the character of Hamlet, proceeds to general observations on the ghost, projects a comparison between Hamlet's "action" and Medea's, attempts to justify the jests made by Hamlet, and concludes with a note on the state of Englishmen from Shakespeare's time up to the nineteenth century, where the heroic was epitomized by the Iron Duke, Wellington.[74] Interestingly, the report made by Collier (a member of Coleridge's audience) does not cover much of what Coleridge's own notes project, but does indicate that Coleridge, in the case of Hamlet's character, did use the notes in his lecture.[75]

At no point, however, does Coleridge subject the play to a systematic analysis of it as drama per se. Concern with genre was the concern of the "Ancients," of Aristotle and his progeny, the eighteenth-century Neo-classical critics. In the commentary on *Hamlet*, Coleridge disregards concern for genre when he disregards the "dramatic unities." He demonstrates in his own preoccupation with interpretation of character his disregard for the "dramatic unities" so much revered by the preceding century. Occasionally brilliant, usually provocative, Coleridge's Shakespearean criticism may be said to suggest rather than to conclude. This habit of suggestion is in keeping with his two major critical tenets: "organic unity" and "reconciliation of opposites." In the former, the work of art must constantly be growing and becoming;[76] therefore, conclusions must always be tentative only.[77] For these reasons, the best kind of criticism is not judicial or conclusive but suggestive and open-ended. In support of this is the second tenet. For every set of opposites reconciled, the reconciliation effects another set; that is, the third becomes polar to another and therefore urges still further reconciliation. Such constant pushing toward a greater and higher synthesis serves to point up the dynamic in both art and life. In illustration of this, Coleridge cites Shakespeare as possessed of the esemplastic power so essential to this dynamism:

It is Shakespeare's peculiar excellence, that throughout the whole of his splendid picture-gallery . . . we find individuality everywhere, mere portrait nowhere. In all his various characters, we feel ourselves communing with the same nature, which is everywhere present as the vegetable sap in the branches, sprays, leaves, buds, blossoms, and fruits, their shapes, tastes, and odors. Speaking of the effect, that is, his works themselves, we may define the excellence of their method as consisting in that just proportion, that union and interpenetration, of the universal and the particular, which must ever pervade all works of decided genius and true science.[78]

The reconciliation of the particular with the general, the individual with the universal, is to Coleridge a consummation devoutly to be wished. While Johnson may stress Shakespeare's ability to convey the universal and may frown upon any concern for the individual, Coleridge sees Shakespeare's greatness in his ability to reconcile the two. He is the master who realizes "multeity in unity," as Coleridge puts it. This means that Shakespeare has the ability to shape the many into the one and yet to retain the sanctity of essential parts in relation to the whole. He does this not mechanistically but organically, as the above quotation indicates. The difference in point of view between the criticism of Johnson and that of Coleridge receives attention in the following statement by Walter Jackson Bate: "The reality that we call 'nature' in short, is neither to be found in the particular, the concrete, by itself, apart from the form, nor in the universal by itself. Instead, the reality of nature is to be found in a *process*, or activity, in which the universal and the particular fulfill each other." [79] Although Johnson would have found reality in the universal by itself, Coleridge found reality, as Bate states, in the combination of the universal and the particular.

In addition to *Hamlet,* Coleridge discussed in some detail *Lear, Macbeth, Othello, Romeo and Juliet, Richard II, The Tempest,* and *Love's Labours Lost.* He of course alluded to many more, but a word on the first six of these should suffice to give some idea of the bent of his remarks.

Although Coleridge seemed to grasp the cosmic greatness of *Lear,* he was never able to explicate it. He saw *Lear* as a play fraught with the kind of power which absorbed all incident in its advance. He saw the tragic action ensuing not from improbability, but from a universal situation ever close to the hearts of men: ". . . parental anguish from filial ingratitude, the genuineness of worth, tho' coffered in bluntness, the vileness of smooth iniquity." [80] He saw *Macbeth* as a fine play, wholly tragic, marred only by the Porter's scenes, which he felt were written by a hand other than Shakespeare's or interpolated by the actors themselves.[81] As Raysor notes, this observation points out Coleridge's intolerance of comic relief in tragedy and once again marks him as a critic interested in the "philosophical" and lyrical aspects of the plays rather than in the dramatic aspects.[82] Two reports of Coleridge's lecture on *Macbeth,* both from the *Bristol Gazette,* indicate that he saw Lady Macbeth as a sensitive woman and not as the monster she was held to be by many former critics.[83] Macbeth himself he likened to Bonaparte, an unrelieved tyrant to whom any means were justified by the end.[84] Coleridge refuted the neoclassical charge that Shakespeare was a primitive genius writing for a barbarous age. He believed that, with the exception of ". . . the trampling out of Gloster's eyes in Lear," Shakespeare does not offend by describing atrocities. In support of this, he cited the sensitive handling of the murder of Lady Macduff and her son.[85] The commentary on *Othello* is much less orthodox than the one on *Macbeth.* Coleridge attempted to show that Othello did not have a jealous nature.[86] He believed Othello's weakness lay in his primitive simplicity which left the Moor unable to cope with the more sophisticated natures around him.[87] Coleridge did not focus upon the quintessential passions which brought about the tragedy. He spent his time discussing whether or not Othello was a Negro (finally concluding that he was not) and in examining the "passionless character" of Iago.[88]

His criticism of *Romeo and Juliet* provides a brilliant discussion of and justification for that work. Coleridge was fully aware that *Romeo and Juliet* was not one of the great tragedies, but that it was one which included ". . . all of the crude materials of future excellence." [89] To Coleridge's mind, the play had to be numbered among the lesser tragedies because it had a less happy combination of parts than that apparent in some of the later tragedies. Coleridge again used the analogy of the tree to convey meaning; the play, for example, had the ". . . limbs of giant growth; but the production, as a whole, in which each part gives delight for itself, and the whole, consisting of these delightful parts, communicates the highest intellectual pleasure and satisfaction, is the result of the application of judgement and taste." [90] These latter elements, he believed, were not fully exercised in *Romeo and Juliet*. For this reason, the play was less tragic than the great tragedies.

Turning to some of the specific critical comments made on the play, Coleridge found Mercutio to be ". . . one of our poet's truly Shakespearian characters." [91] To Coleridge, Mercutio seemed to be drawn wholly from imagination and not at all from observation. Coleridge found the nurse to be a great deal more than the aggregate of the poet's memory, the creature of mere observation. He saw her to be a splendid combination of ignorance, grossness, affection, and capriciousness.[92] As for the permanent and violent passion of Romeo and Juliet themselves, Coleridge saw this as not only wholly justifiable, but also as admirable. If love is, as Plato defined it, the desire of the half to become united with another being in order to complete itself, then Romeo and Juliet were lovers in accord with the ideal of love.[93] Shakespeare, in having Romeo sigh for Rosaline in the opening lines of the play, has drawn the fine distinction between a young man in love with the ideal of love and later, when love is realized in the person of Juliet, a young man in love with love incarnate in a human being. Once the idea or ideal of love was fixed in Romeo's mind (as it was in the Rosaline interlude), then he is ready to have the ideal realized, for he has now " . . . felt that necessity of being beloved which no noble mind can be without." [94]

The lyric power of *Richard II* intrigued Coleridge. He saw the play as ". . . the summit of excellence in the delineation and preservation of character." [95] In a discussion of the character of Richard, Coleridge pinpointed his weakness as a constitutional femininity. In view of this trait, Richard did not seem to Coleridge to be the debauched, malevolent character that some critics saw him to be, but rather one who wore the garments of a king but who possessed the spine of a weakling. Richard's lack of manliness seemed to Coleridge to lie at the root of his destruction. Rather than ruler of, he was subject to, flattery. He held no energy in reserve but let himself give way to the "Constant overflow of feelings." [96] Hamlet was too thoughtful; Richard was too weak.

The Tempest received more of Coleridge's attention than *Love's Labours Lost.* He used the play as a frame of reference within which to order his sallies against both the French and the neo-classical schools of criticism. The latter supported the point of view that the drama, as specific genre, was to be a copy of nature. So viewed, the drama was not at all deceptive, but was a re-enactment of actual life. The former, the French school, saw the drama not as copy or re-enactment but as the thing itself, that is, as *life.* Coleridge believed both points of view to be erroneous. He saw the drama as neither the copy of reality nor as reality itself, but as a skilful "illusion" or "imitation" which the audience is for the moment willing to accept.[97] *The Tempest* itself was to Coleridge the most imaginative of all the plays: ". . . [it] addresses itself entirely to the imaginative faculty." [98] Prospero himself is utterly believable because of the reconciliation within him of head and heart, a quality which makes him credible as extraordinary seer and ordinary father.[99]

Coleridge also commented on Shakespeare's poetry, which to him was the precursor of the drama. In *Venus and Adonis* and the *Rape of Lucrece,* Coleridge saw Shakespeare's "creative power" to be at war with his "intellectual energy"; each stood as a threat to the other. When these opposites became reconciled, the result was Shakespeare's drama.[100]

To read Coleridge's summary comments on Shakespeare is nearly to recapitulate his summation of the essential Wordsworth. Shakespeare, like Wordsworth, is a poet of high imaginative genius.[101] He has tremendous lyric power welling up out of his poetic nature, out of his "deep feeling and exquisite sense of beauty." In addition, he has that ". . . affectionate love of nature and natural objects, without which no man could have observed so steadily, or painted so truly and passionately the very minutest of the external world." [102] Like Wordsworth in this respect, Shakespeare is like him also in his philosophical power.[103] The point of difference between the two lies in Shakespeare's superior handling of fancy.[104] In a final word, Coleridge states that Shakespeare would have been able to stand on his poetry alone had he never written the dramas. He has the distinction of being, ". . . the only modern poet who was both a poet and at the same time a dramatic poet." [105]

The criticism of Wordsworth and Shakespeare, while composing the largest and most significant parts of Coleridge's criticism, is by no means his only critical commentary. He had something to say about almost every literary figure, ancient and modern. Some of what he had to say is fairly easy to predict, for it reflects his affinity with the Romantic school of criticism. Of Southey, for example, his long-suffering friend, relative, and benefactor, Coleridge spoke highly. It was the man himself, however, whom he praised. Occasionally apologetic for Southey's work, Coleridge rationalized, saying that after all Southey had so many responsibilities and such a strong sense of duty that he could not always fulfill his poetic promise.[106] The critic's involvement with the character of the poet, rather than with his work alone, has been considered from the modern critical point of view a specifically modern trait.

Coleridge gave but little praise to most of the poetry of the eighteenth century. He saw Pope's *Rape of the Lock* as a poem addressed only to the fancy; and the *Essay on Man* as a poem addressed only to the intellect. He found lacking in much of the poetry of the eighteenth century that reconciliation of head with heart which was so greatly to be desired. In addition, he believed much of the poetry of this era to be no poetry at all, but merely ". . . translations of prose thoughts into poetic language," productive therefore of many terse epigrams of small consequence and no heart.[107]

It would be impossible to list all of Coleridge's likes and dislikes with respect to authors, but below are a few names which show the range of his opinions. Milton and Dante he admired very much and felt they came closest to Shakespeare in "picturesque power." [108] He thought the comedies of Beaumont and Fletcher exquisite,[109] the stories of Boccaccio entertaining.[110] He liked such narrative masters as Homer (the *Odyssey* over the *Iliad*) [111] and Fielding.[112]

Coleridge disliked, in varying degrees, Donne, Richardson, Voltaire, Ariosto, Tasso, Campbell, and others previously mentioned.[113] Primarily, his dislikes were based upon his belief that poetry should reconcile head with heart and should be imaginative and morally uplifting.

In the main Coleridge's literary criticism is exciting. It provokes, it challenges, it annoys. The fragmentary nature of much of it, the labyrinthian character of the prose itself, plus the appreciative mode of approach make it almost impossible to analyze systematically. Nonetheless, Coleridge's own love of *belles-lettres* is infectious and nowhere more obvious than in the literary criticism. A substantial amount of reading in this body of Coleridge's writing will serve to leave the reader not only more knowledgeable concerning Coleridge's specific approach and more aware of some of the characteristics of the Romantic mode of criticism, but also more deeply appreciative of some of the great writers of the Western world.

CHAPTER 9

The Prose: Philosophical Writings

IF the *Biographia Literaria* is one of the chief repositories of Coleridge's criticism, it is also of paramount importance in any study of his philosophical writings. For the general reader, a study of the *Biographia* and of *Aids to Reflection* should suffice to indicate the broad outlines of Coleridge's philosophical point of view. These volumes, however, while germane to such a study, are nonetheless representative of only a small part of the vast amount of philosophical pronouncements which Coleridge left to posterity. Unfortunately, the philosophical writings are even less well organized than the literary criticism, are often fragmentary, and are never truly systematic. Professor Alice Snyder was correct in her contention that Coleridge had a philosophical standpoint rather than a system.[1] But this standpoint is not one which can be explicated with any degree of consistency, for it changed like a chameleon from the early years to the later. It has already been pointed out that Coleridge moved from associationism, necessitarianism, and like mechanistic philosophies, to something which bordered on philosophical idealism. But Coleridge himself was not content to be labeled a follower of either camp. In the *Biographia*, he discussed this matter at some length. Again the accent is on method, as it was formerly in the literary criticism. The epistemological branch of philosophy captivated him and, for the moment, pushed aside both ontology and ethics. He had this to say concerning what might appear to be antithetical, objective versus subjective:

Now the sum of all that is merely OBJECTIVE we will henceforth call NATURE, confining the term to its passive and material sense, as comprising all the phaenomena by which its existence is made known to us. On the other hand the sum of all that is SUBJECTIVE, we may comprehend in the name of the SELF or INTELLIGENCE. Both conceptions are in necessary antithesis. Intelligence is conceived of as exclusively representative, nature as exclusively represented; the one as conscious, the other as without consciousness. Now in all acts of positive knowledge there is required a reciprocal concurrence of both, namely of the conscious being, and of that which is in itself unconscious. Our problem is to explain this concurrence, its possibility and its necessity.[2]

For Coleridge, the very act of knowledge presupposes a commingling of objective and subjective to the extent that neither can be singly identified. He does, however, for purposes of elucidation, attempt to separate the two. He looks at objectivism as a way of knowing and finds it lacking. For those who subscribe to this approach to the nature of reality, a desk exists whether there is anyone to behold it or not. He says, "This then is the problem of natural philosophy. It assumes the objective or unconscious nature as the first, and has therefore to explain how intelligence can supervene to it, or how itself can grow into intelligence." [3] Then he discusses subjectivism, specifically subjective idealism. To use the same illustration, there would be no desk without a beholder to behold it. Coleridge finds this approach to the nature of reality also lacking. In order to resolve the two, he resorts to his own method, the reconciliation of opposites. He seeks to arrive at a synthesis between the two approaches, to discover a more accurate approach to the nature of reality than is to be found either in a mechanistic objectivism or in an idealistic subjectivism:

The realism common to all mankind is far elder and lies infinitely deeper than this hypothetical explanation of the origin of our perceptions, an explanation skimmed from the mere surface of mechanical philosophy. . . . [and] If to destroy the reality of all, that we actually behold, be idealism, what can be more egregiously so, than the system of modern metaphysics, which banishes us to a land of shadows, surrounds us with apparitions, and distinguishes truth from illusion only by the majority of those who dream the same dream? [Therefore] It is to the true and original realism, that I would direct the attention. This believes and requires neither more nor less, than the object which it beholds or presents to itself, is the real and very object.[4]

In Coleridge's opinion, all men are born collectively idealists, ". . . and therefore and only therefore are [they] at the same time realists." [5] From this belief he evolved the construct Reason and Understanding, itself a concomitant of his equally famous construct, Imagination and Fancy. To explain the existence of the material world, while still reserving the right to believe in the immaterial or spiritual world, has ever been a challenge to interested men. To the Romantics, some resolution of the dilemma was imperative. Coleridge, above all other Romantics, most successfully seemed to resolve the antithetical points of view. He accomplished this by ascribing to the mind two faculties, or two kinds of thinking: reason and understanding. He believed that a comprehension of both terms and their differential operation was absolutely essential to the handling of philosophy and its concepts.[6] In the *Aids to Reflection*[7] he discourses on the difference in kind between these two ways of knowing. First of all, he divides the reason into two aspects as he had earlier divided imagination into two: "Contemplated distinctively in reference to formal (or abstract) truth, it is the Speculative Reason; but in reference to actual (or moral) truth, as the fountain of ideas and the light of conscience, we name it the Practical Reason." [8]

Taken together, as a whole, however: "Reason is the power of universal and necessary convictions, the source and substance of truths above sense, and having their evidence in themselves. Its presence is always marked by the necessity of the position affirmed: this necessity being conditional, when a truth of reason is applied to facts of experience, or to the rules and maxims of the understanding; but absolute, when the subject matter is itself the growth or offspring of reason." [9]

Whenever man subjects himself to the light of reason, which is a universal light, his particular will becomes one with the will of reason and he is then "regenerate" and thereby ". . . capable of a quickening intercommunion with the Divine Spirit." [10] Hence reason may be equated with that which is spirit in man, that which differentiates him from animals, and that which allies him directly with God. It is reason, for example, which enables man to know that all things in this world have unity even though they appear separate and discrete. Coleridge, in *Aids*, uses the metaphor of a house with many mansions. That there is no owner in sight does not presuppose no owner exists, for the aggregate of objects without a subject would be nonsense.[11] And again, the fact that the mass of men wander about and "have no certain harbor" and know not what they seek does not prove that there is nothing worthy of being sought.[12] Reason is a kind of cosmic stabilizer, at one and the same time the anchor and wings of mankind enabling him to keep with perfect tenor that balance requisite to wholeness.

The understanding is "'the faculty judging according to sense.'" Here Coleridge lets a definitional phrase from Leighton stand for what he himself means. The objects of man's senses are those which are of concern to the understanding.[13] For example, the common-sense man, or he who is governed by understanding alone, is a total materialist (objectivist). For him, a desk exists, without doubt, independent of a thinker or beholder. Poetry, when it is the product of fancy only, is also the product of understanding only, rather than the product of imagination and reason. In consequence, the poetry initiating in the fancy and understanding is greatly inferior to the poetry of high imagination. For the man governed solely by understanding, life is lived at a sensuous and often sensual level similar to that lived by the beasts of the field. The judgments of the understanding enable man to operate up to a point in this world, the common-sense world; but they do not enable him to envision the next. Indeed, even animals are possessed of understanding, which differs in degree from animal to man, but not in kind. Witness the industry and progress of the ant, cited by Coleridge in reference to Huber's *Natural History of Ants*.[14] Animals, on the other hand, do not have the faculty of reason. One should not speak of human *reason*, for this would be tautological. "There neither is nor can be but one reason, one and the same," [15] and this reason is the chief inheritance of man from God.

Coleridge himself clarifies the two faculties within the construct by setting two columns side by side which enumerate the respective functions of each:[16]

Understanding	*Reason*
1. Understanding is discursive.	1. Reason is fixed.
2. The Understanding in all its judgments refers to some other faculty as its ultimate authority.	2. The Reason in all its decisions appeals to itself as the ground and *substance* of their truth. (*Heb.* vi. 13.)
3. Understanding is the faculty of reflection.	3. Reason of contemplation . . .

In addition to these columns is the example which Coleridge himself uses to demonstrate the differential functions of understanding and reason, the latter at its practical level: He states that the Ptolemaic theory of the universe relied exclusively upon the function of the understanding, whereas the Newtonian depended in part upon the function of the reason.

He also applies the construct to talent and genius: "Talent, lying in the understanding, is often inherited; genius, being the action of reason and imagination, rarely or never." [17] As the fancy deals with fixities and definites, so the understanding deals with objects of sense; and thus the equation, imagination is to the fancy as reason is to the understanding, is a reliable one. How does reason relate to imagination? As Fogle states, the primary imagination is the instrument of Coleridge's psychology and philosophy, while the secondary imagination is the instrument of his criticism.[18] In actuality, the speculative reason is directly allied with the primary imagination, whereas the practical reason is directly allied with the secondary imagination. Neither differs in kind from the other, but simply with respect to the function appropriate to each. The real difference exists between the imagination and the fancy, and between the reason and the understanding. In a multiplicity of ways Coleridge employs these constructs, but in the philosophical writings it is to the latter construct, reason and understanding, that he devotes his attention. The relationship, however, between the two constructs is an intimate one, and is therefore not to be lost sight of.

Another construct or principle which appears again and again in Coleridge's philosophical writings is the "principle of individuation." This principle has already been seen in Coleridge's discussion of Shakespeare's greatness which is explicable in terms of the extent to which he demonstrates it in operation. In an essay as abstruse as any which Coleridge wrote, "Hints towards the Formation of a more Comprehensive Theory of Life," [19] this principle assumes first importance. This brief essay attempts to do exactly what the title states, to present directions toward a theory of life. "To *account* for Life is one thing: to explain Life another," [20] wrote Coleridge, indicating his conviction that although science attempted the former, there was great need for the latter. For Coleridge, life is ". . . *the principle of individuation,* or the power which unites a given *all* into a *whole* that is presupposed by all its parts." [21] Again, the accent is upon power. Imagination is a power; reason is a power; and the principle of individuation is similarly a power. That which might be categorized as a tendency to individuation is this power operating to combine the whole with its parts. And this tendency quite obviously calls into operation another principle, that of the "reconciliation of opposites" pushing ever outward and onward to a greater and greater synthesis. In this respect, Coleridge's theory of life is an evolutionary one, intimately allied of course with the principle operating in his literary criticism, that of "organic unity." For example, the power which stirs in the bird has been latent in the egg, and so on in endless progression. [22]

In the lower animals and vegetable world this power of individuation is operative; in man the power has reached a zenith but not an ultimate nor a stopping point. In man ". . . the individuality is not only perfected in its corporeal sense, but begins a new series beyond the appropriate limits of physiology." [23] As Coleridge explains:

Life, then, we consider as the copula, or the unity of thesis and antithesis, position and counterposition.—Life itself being the positive of both; as, on the other hand, the two counterpoints are the necessary conditions of the *manifestations* of Life. These, by the same necessity, unite in a synthesis; which again, by the law of dualism, essential to all actual existence, expands, or *produces* itself, from the point into the *line,* in order again to converge, as the initiation of the same productive process in some intenser form of reality. Thus, in the identity of the two counter-powers, Life *sub*sists; in their strife it *con*sists: and in their reconciliation it at once dies and is born again into a new form, either falling back into the life of the whole, or starting anew in the process of individuation. [24]

It is quite easy to see the organic, dynamic, and evolutionary aspects of such a theory; and it is almost equally simple to recognize the inter-relationships between such a theory and its integral constructs: imagination and reason.

Coleridge's interest in method and process, demonstrated in the chapters on poetry and literary criticism, is seen also in his philosophical pronouncements. In the conclusion to the essay, "Theory of Life," he sees life not as a thing, a something fixed or definite, but rather as a process, an act, a growing and becoming: ". . .

Life itself is not a *thing*—a self-subsistent *hypostasis*—but an *act* and *process;* which, pitiable as the prejudice will appear to the *forts esprits*, is a great deal more than either my reason would authorize or my conscience allow me to assert—concerning the Soul, as the principle both of Reason and Conscience." [25]

Briefly then, Coleridge, in his philosophical writings, is as interested in pointing up "method" as he was in the literary criticism. To this end, the principles he emphasizes are: "organic unity," "reconciliation of opposites," "individuation," and the construct, "reason and understanding."

I *The Philosophical Writings per se*

At least one half of the *Biographia* is devoted to a discussion of Coleridge's philosophical orientation, while all of the *Aids to Reflection* is involved with a discussion of his own philosophical and religious beliefs. The purpose of *Aids* was to give spiritual and moral assistance to those who wished to cultivate a disciplined mind and life.[26] Specifically, the volume was directed to young men interested in the Christian ministry.[27] Coleridge's plan of organization for the book was to show the distinct characters of prudence, morality, and religion and to establish the large distinction between reason and understanding, so essential to any who would lead the good life and reconcile others to that end. As usual with Coleridge, no single purpose would suffice. For this reason, the over-all concern seems to be what might well be considered his constant concern, the reconciliation of philosophy with religion.

In the *Aids*, there is a progression from introductory aphorisms, through prudential aphorisms, moral and religious aphorisms, elements of religious philosophy, to aphorisms on spiritual religion Commentary on the distinction between the reason and understanding, on instinct, original sin, redemption, and baptism concludes the work. Needless to say, such a plan indicates a veritable grab bag of subject material. But as usual with Coleridge, the grab bag is not filled with minutiae but rather with vast imponderables, the like of which at one and the same time frustrate and challenge the reader, but which do have nonetheless a loose relationship to one another.

Although it would be impossible here to discuss the nature of all of these imponderables, one such is the nature of morality. For Coleridge, morality has religious overtones: "Morality is the body, of which the faith in Christ is the soul." [28] The duties of morality are namely of two kinds. One is *negative* and isolate: to keep oneself pure, isolating oneself from the corrupting influences of the world. The other is *positive:* to spread good will and good works among mankind.[29] By exercising these antithetical duties, an ascent takes place from "uprightness" to "Godlikeness." Such an ascent is in keeping with the great and divine design for man's redemption and "second creation or birth in the divine image." [30] Thus even within the very nature of morality opposites exist and strive to become reconciled in a progressively higher third. Therefore, from prudence which corresponds to the heart and conscience in man, to the spiritual which corresponds to the will and finite reason (in man), which in turn has a greater correspondence with Reason and Will infinite (Absolute),[31] Coleridge attempts to view the whole man, his several functions and capacities, and his great potential. In so doing, he does set before these young men, who anticipate a career in the ministry, certain aids to reflection. He also demonstrates by so doing several ways in which Reason and Christianity can be reconciled.[32] Another "aid" with which he concerns himself is a consideration of the nature of the Will. In the section entitled "Elements of Religious Philosophy" which is primarily allied with his section on "Spiritual Religion," Coleridge attributes to the Will in man properties of spirituality. He makes the statement that ". . . there is more in man than can be rationally referred to the life of nature and the mechanism of organization," [33] a statement which clearly shows his own affinity for the philosophy of idealism. That something "more" is Will and it is ". . . in an especial and pre-eminent sense the spiritual part of our humanity." [34] Again, the Will is a power, not an object or a thing per se. The question might be raised, "What is the difference between Will and Reason?" And the answer would have to be "very little." Will cannot be separated from Reason, for both are that in man which differentiates him from all else. In point of fact, the difference is almost absurdly a moot point. When Coleridge is talking about philosophy, he uses the term *Reason.* When he is talking about religion, he uses the term *Will.* Both Reason and Will have their origin in God. Both are at one and the same time autonomous from, and subject to, their source. This was not something which Coleridge could prove; therefore, he threw the matter back on each individual:

I utterly disclaim the notion, that any human intelligence, with whatever power it might manifest itself, is alone adequate to the office of restoring health to the will: but at the same time I deem it impious and absurd to hold that the Creator would have given us the faculty of reason, or that the Redeemer would in so many varied forms of argument and persuasion have appealed to it, if it had been either totally useless or wholly impotent. Lastly, I find all these several truths reconciled and united in the belief, that the imperfect human understanding can be effectually exerted only in subordination to, and in a dependent alliance with, the means and aidances supplied by the All-perfect and Supreme Reason; but that under these conditions it is not only an admissible, but a necessary instrument of bettering both ourselves and others.[35]

The twentieth century does not hold with such "philosophizing," but in the nineteenth God was still held (in many circles) to be an a priori fact. Because of this, Coleridge's mode of thought did not meet with severe rebuttal, though his mode of discourse often met with severe criticism.

Although *Table Talk* is in many respects a veritable compendium of minutiae, it serves to show the extent to which Coleridge's informal conversations ranged over the subjects of philosophy and religion. *Table Talk* is a posthumous report by Henry N. Coleridge (the poet's nephew) of Coleridge's conversations, as the former remembered them. It was Henry Coleridge's purpose to assist the reader in gaining insight into ". . . the great and pregnant principles, in the light of which Mr. Coleridge was accustomed to regard God and the World." [36] By this time, it is easy to see that Coleridge's prose does indeed refer continually to his beloved "philosophical" and religious principles; and *Table Talk* is no exception. On the other hand, the range of subject includes snippets of an extraordinary number of topics. The following list, by no means all-inclusive, suggests this range: personalities of the day, literary criticism, philosophy, Christianity per se, the Church of Rome, religion in general, dreams, science, flora and fauna, grammar, flogging, political science, logic, the English government, ghosts, dancing, marriage, the idea of freedom, history, education, and so on. According to Henry Coleridge, any inability of the reader or listener to follow Coleridge's writings or conversations was not the fault of Coleridge but rather of the reader-listener himself.[37] Perhaps so, but to read *Table Talk* from cover to cover requires mental gymnastics of Olympian dexterity.

Among the more illuminating of the philosophical pronouncements is Coleridge's statement that he wished to ". . . reduce all knowledges into harmony." [38] To this end, he stated, he has examined all systems of philosophy, clarified each, and found each to contain but half truth. This half in each he has sought to reconcile with the truth of other and still other systems, and so on in an almost infinite process of synthesis. Ultimately, it was of course his hope to produce that "whole," so much touted by him in the *Biographia*, that is the *Logosophia*, his own projected comprehensive system of philosophy. The fact that Coleridge never produced any such work did not deter him from talking about it endlessly.[39] *Table Talk*, for all the rambling nature of its subject material, contains but a portion of the conversational snippets collected by Henry N. Coleridge.

The *Anima Poetae*, like *Table Talk*, is another posthumous collection of the poet's notes, marginalia, taken from the beginning of his literary career up until 1828. Edited by another distinguished relative, Ernest Hartley Coleridge, grandson of the poet, it is a kind of extension of the same aphoristic treatment which characterized the earlier *Table Talk*. The contents of the *Anima Poetae* are roughly organized by subject in the margin of the text and range from commentary on infants and infancy to the "embryonic soul" and "abstract self." [40] The contribution of this volume is of course now being superseded by the editing in full of all of the notebooks by Kathleen Coburn. The *Anima Poetae* will continue to be of use to the student who has neither the time nor the need to wrestle with the complete text of the notebooks. In the *Anima Poetae*, as might be expected, there are many snippets which pertain to Coleridge's religious and philosophical beliefs. Two of these support those ever-present first principles. Coleridge states that the One and the Good early appeared to him, and that he realized even in his youth that they were God.[41] In another place, he gives the kernel of his pervasive belief that each part and particle is capable of yielding up the characteristics of the whole. For example, the single drop of water, when subjected to microscopic study, yields knowledge of motion, tumult, struggle, and life.[42] Both *Table Talk* and *Anima Poetae* were well received by the public. It was not that the death of Coleridge had left any sacrosanct aura to his work, but rather that these two collections were presented in an informal, social style, and were in consequence more palatable to those who encountered them than were some of the more turgid philosophical writings.

Among Coleridge's more thoughtful prose writings are the *Lay Sermons,* the first published in 1816, and the second in 1817.[43] The two lay sermons are addressed to an English audience of those two years (in particular to the upper and middle classes in England as the title page to the second *Sermon* would indicate) for the purpose of setting before it such conditions as Coleridge fervently felt needed amelioration where possible and abolishment where necessary. Again emphasizing the essentiality of men's operating in the light of principles, Coleridge addresses these upper strata of English society, urging them to raise their sights and contemplate what lies above mere temporal facts, to strive to realize these first principles and thereby to act in accordance with their duty as men. He makes the point that whereas men used to be worse than their principles, now principles appear worse than men.[44] He further admonishes the upper classes, whose greater rank and privilege carry with them concomitant greater responsibilities, to look not to common sense, honesty, genius, talent, or learning alone, but rather "to walk in the light" of their own knowledge, thereby resisting the impulse to follow the crowd blindly.[45] Having indicated to men the way, he then indicates what needs improvement. He believes, and says, that Englishmen pay too much attention to material gain and temporal talent, to the detriment of any recognition of and realization of eternal verities.[46] Men, he states, in the England of his day would choose a craftsman over Plato, were the latter suddenly to appear.[47] He sees men as not only uninterested in philosophy and religion, but also as actually hostile to them and to that which eludes the mere faculty of understanding. In philosophy, men's distrust is leveled specifically against metaphysics, and men's trust centers upon only that which can be seen.[48] In religion, men's distrust of abstruse philosophy takes the form of Unitarianism, a form more readily acceptable to modern men's mechanistically oriented natures[49] because the humanity rather than the divinity of Christ receives emphasis. Also allied to the religious decline in England, he remarks, is the deplorable state of preaching. To Coleridge, any six sermons of Donne or Taylor would be more challenging than a year's sermons by any contemporary divine.[50] The remedy for the present moral and religious crisis in England is summed up in this statement: "We must learn to act nationally as well as individually, as Christians. We must remove half truths, the most dangerous of errors . . . [and replace them] by the whole truth." [51]

A third "Lay Sermon" makes up the content of *The Statesman's Manual* and is generally known by that title.[52] This sermon is addressed to the upper class only and expounds the idea that the *Bible* contains those principles most appropriate to guide men in political skill and foresight.[53] Coleridge makes the point that in times of peace and prosperity men seem content to operate on the basis of facts and particular truths, that is, on the things of the understanding alone; but in times of war and stress, men seek out those principles of first importance which are known to the reason alone.[54] The best repository for that Supreme Reason, ". . . whose knowledge is creative, and antecedent to the things known, as distinguished from the understanding, or creaturely mind of the individual, the acts of which are posterior to the things which it records and arranges," rests within the Holy Scriptures.[55] One of the foremost reasons for the solidarity of the Jewish Church and law is that those who were united under it drew ". . . their particular rules and prescripts . . . directly and visibly from universal principles." [56]

Aids to Reflection, Table Talk, Anima Poetae, and the *Lay Sermons* all concern themselves to greater or lesser degrees with those principles, and the method by which they are realized, so characteristic of, and essential to, the life of Reason in man. Another treatise, perhaps even more deeply concerned with principles, but much less well accepted by the public are the essays which make up Coleridge's periodical, *The Friend.*[57] In this series of essays, Coleridge states that his main concern was for ". . . what we are and what we are born to become." [58] The essays contained therein are confusing to the point of distraction, a fact of no great wonder in view of the ambitious purposes of their author. According to Coleridge, the object and plan of the work was ". . . to assist the mind in the formation for itself of sound, and therefore permanent and universal, principles in regard to the investigation, perception, and retention of truth, in what direction soever it may be pursued." [59] These directions were mainly three: men as citizens of state (in the area of politics), as "men to our neighbors" (in the realm of morality), and as "creatures to our Creator," in the realm of religion.[60]

Such a vast scope seemed to predestine the failure that resulted. To add to the confusion dictated by the purpose is the fact that Coleridge chose to apportion men and nations among four categories: Genius, Talent, Sense, and Cleverness. In support of this dubious classification, he chose to range through all history and creation for his examples. Before examining his classification, some idea of his definitions of these terms must be given. To him, Men of Genius were those characterized by ". . . originality in intellectual construction; the moral accompaniment, and actuating principle of which consists, perhaps, in the carrying on of the freshness and feelings of childhood into the powers of manhood." [61] The Man of Talent was distinguished by that ". . . comparative facility of acquiring, arranging, and applying the stock furnished by others, and already existing in books or other conservatories of intellect." [62] The Man of Sense was he who maintained ". . . that just balance of the faculties which is to the judgment what health is to the body . . . The general accompaniment of sense is a disposition to avoid extremes, whether in theory or in practice, with a desire to remain in sympathy with the general mind of the age or country, and a feeling of the necessity and utility of compromise." [63] The Man of Cleverness, finally, was he who demonstrated ". . . a comparative readiness in the invention and use of means, for the realizing of objects and ideas—often of such ideas, which the man of genius only could have originated, and which the clever man perhaps neither fully comprehends nor adequately appreciates, even at the moment that he is prompting or executing the machinery of their accomplishment." [64] While it is comparatively easy to see the direction of Coleridge's thought in establishing these definitions, they make little sense when practically applied to establish categories. For example, when applied to countries, the breakdown is as specious and nonsensical as the following examples indicate:

Germany: Genius, Talent, Fancy (here wild ornamentation)
England: Genius, Sense, Humor
France: Cleverness, Talent, Wit[65]

Inasmuch as Genius is the most desirable of the qualities, it is easy to see why Coleridge admired Germany and England over France. The following two quotations establish his prejudice and summarize the point of view: "If genius be the initiative, and talent the administrative, sense is the conservative, branch in the intellectual republic." [66] Applied to literature, ". . . cleverness is more frequently accompanied by wit, genius and sense by humor." [67] These categories quite obviously have no intrinsic worth, but they do serve to show Coleridge's continuing delight with definition and classification.

Not only was Coleridge interested in principles per se and with ways and means of establishing and supporting them, but he was also interested in the ways and means of realizing them. Therefore, *The Friend* incorporates within it Coleridge's theory of the science of method. Coleridge believed that by examining certain philosophical systems each man might be able to find truth according to the principles and guidelines set forth through such an examination.[68] He believed that the well-disciplined mind evidenced in its approach to truth a necessarily strong reliance upon the science of method.[69] This awareness of method was a characteristic which Shakespeare always demonstrated, and such is that which distinguishes the educated man from the uneducated. The uneducated have no method in their approach, but rather find truth by mere accident if they find it at all.[70] But the educated man shows by his conversation that he anticipates with words the whole, that is from ". . . unpremeditated and evidently habitual arrangement of his words, grounded on the habit of foreseeing, in each integral part . . . in every sentence, the whole that he then intends to communicate." [71] In this way, ". . . all method supposes a union of several things to a common end." [72]

With respect to method, Coleridge believed that there were two ways of contemplating the objects of the mind. First of all, one could arrive at them by assuming that certain principles, hypotheses, or theorems existed a priori and thus controlled the objects of the mind. Secondly, one could see these objects as they appear as objects qua objects, and from their relationships to one another one could arrive at that which existed as a governing principle.[73] It is not difficult to see that a redaction of Coleridge's two ways of contemplating the objects of the mind would yield the two philosophical methods: deductive versus inductive reasoning. For

Coleridge, the first is that of *law* ". . . which, in its absolute perfection, is conceivable only of the Supreme Being, whose creative idea not only appoints to each thing its position, but in that position, and in consequence of that position, gives it its qualities . . . its very existence, as that particular thing." [74] The second or inductive approach produces on the other hand only ". . . schemes conducive to the peculiar purposes of particular sciences." [75] This second method is that ". . . theory, in which existing forms and qualities of objects, discovered by observation or experiment, suggest a given arrangement of many under one point of view." [76] For Coleridge, Plato in his advocacy of the Doctrine of Ideas would stand as an exponent of the first method, while Aristotle might be considered an exponent of the second.[77] It was the purpose of Plato's works ". . . to establish the sources, to evolve the principles, and exemplify the art of method." [78] Similarly Coleridge hoped to urge men to approach truth. One way to do this was for man to recognize nature in himself: ". . . man must first learn to comprehend nature in himself, and its laws in the ground of his own existence." [79] Once this was accomplished, he would be able to ". . . reduce phaenomena to principles," [80] and thus the science of method becomes integral to his approach.

Always fond of antitheses, Coleridge again demonstrates this affection in *The Friend*. In man, an essential polarity resides within the intellect. This ". . . dialectic intellect by the exertion of its own powers exclusively can lead us to a general affirmation of the supreme reality of an absolute being." [81] As these contrary forces operate in man to produce a third affirmation, so they operate in nations. Nations depend upon man's desire for trade and literature for their very vitality as nations.[82] Both complement man: trade, by having as its object the fulfilment of the wants of the body; and literature, by having as its object the fulfilment of the wants of the mind.[83] The dynamism of this thesis-antithesis-synthesis construct is manifest in Coleridge's contention that the human species continues to progress toward highest truth, not necessarily that each man continues to progress (though certain individuals may and do), but rather that humanity in general does. This progression is not, however, historically uninterrupted. It has its setbacks from time to time. In the over-all view, however, the progression is steadily upward.

Some of the general characteristics of Coleridge's prose writings have already been discussed. The subject of Coleridge as a prose writer is a difficult one to settle, for he is at least two writers in the prose, as he is similarly two poets in his poetry. His prose is, on the one hand, the easy, pithy, aphoristic style of *Table Talk* and *Anima Poetae,* and, on the other hand, the weighty, pontifical, and often circumlocutory style of *The Friend, Aids to Reflection,* and "Toward a Theory of Life." The two styles are, of course, combined in the *Biographia Literaria.* Another major problem, and this exists in both styles, is the enormous amount of repetition from work to work. The repetition of idea has been demonstrated, but there is also repetition of phraseology. Coleridge's habit of breaking off thoughts, sometimes never to return for completion was previously discussed, but a far more grievous problem is that when he does complete the thought, the reader often has difficulty understanding what has been said. Some of this confusion resides within the abstract nature of the subject material itself, but much of it lies in the nature of the prose. The following sentence, one of no great profundity, illustrates the necessity for rereading in order to absorb what has been said: "We are—and, till its good purposes, which are many, have been all achieved, and we can become something better, long may we continue such!—a busy, enterprising and commercial nation." [84] Such "stuffed" sentences scarcely make for easy reading, and Coleridge's prose does abound in them.

As the literary criticism is brilliant, though fragmentary, so the philosophical writings are illuminating, though taxing. No one can hope, however, to comprehend the implications of the concepts of Imagination, Reason, Will, Fancy, Understanding, or Wit; and no one can hope to understand the principles of the reconciliation of opposites, of individuation, and the like, without recourse to Coleridge's philosophical writings. For this reason, these prose works are of prime importance.

CHAPTER 10

Conclusions and Directions

IN the preceding pages, Coleridge has been seen as writer in his various roles of poet, dramatist, literary critic, and philosopher. The following remarks are intended to summarize his contributions briefly and to indicate where further study is needed. He wrote two kinds of poetry that really mattered: the conversation poems and the poems of high imagination. The rest of his poetry, consisting of juvenilia, minor poems, translations, and doggerel verse, yields little that is of significance to any except those who are searching out the developmental aspects of Coleridge's work.

There is still much, however, to be done with the conversation poems, classified as "major minor" in this study. Although they do not, for the most part, make any unique contributions, they are all interesting historically, while a few, "This Lime-tree Bower," "Frost at Midnight," "The Eolian Harp," and the later "Dejection: An Ode," are interesting as poetry per se. In addition, all of the "major minor" poems are interesting in terms of showing Coleridge's development. Often they incorporate his critical theories: organic unity, the reconciliation of opposites, and the like. In this way, they provide background illuminating to the poems of high imagination. Their common characteristics abstracted are as follows: they contain a speaker and a listener; they are usually set in an English rural countryside; and they allude normally with marked respect to the pure in heart. In the better conversation poems, the diction is clear and restrained, the tone serious and measured. There are certain recurrent themes: the fear of the world of men outside the Eden of nature which the speaker and listener inhabit; a desire to remain amid these beauteous forms of nature, although in some of the poems this desire is pitted against a desire to take a Messianic role in the confused world of men. In addition, these poems express a firm belief in the efficacy of na-

ture's beauty and in the existence of a greater Spirit who is benevolently disposed to help those who keep His commandments; and,
finally, the poems treat of man in solitude attempting to justify
the ways of men to men, the only task which remains since the
ways of God to men are clear.

In the less successful of the conversation poems (for example,
"Fears in Solitude") and in most of the minor poems, the sublime
may be touched upon, but it is never wholly realized. These poems
often deteriorate into pontification and hollow rhetoric. They are
also often marred by remnants from another poetic era, namely:
an overuse of personification and classical references from the
seventeenth century, or a certain matter-of-factness carried over
from the eighteenth. These poems, by and large, bespeak the
political-philosophical Coleridge rather than the imaginative poet.
In a manner of speaking, all of the conversation poems can be
said to speak more readily to the Understanding than to the Imagination. Coleridge himself was perfectly aware of this and undoubtedly would have extended to many of them that which he
said concerning "Fears in Solitude," that is, that it was a "kind of
middle thing," neither poetry nor prose.

The poems of high imagination are quite different from the
conversation poems. Harold Bloom prefers to call them poems of
"natural magic," [1] rather than of "high imagination." Regardless
of nomenclature, however, these poems are unique in the sweep
of English poetry. The conversation poems are close to the world
of ordinary men; the poems of high imagination are far removed.
However, although they are set in remote places, either by virtue
of time removal, as in "The Ancient Mariner" and "Christabel," or
by virtue of their distance from an English countryside, as in
"Lewti" and "Kubla Khan," they are closer to quintessential man
by virtue of the truths they reveal. Externally, these poems are
characterized by brilliant imagery, occasionally archaic diction,
and intermittent Gothic touches of horror. They are replete with
supernatural elements or overtones. For the final magic they convey, one must look, however, not solely to externals but to the
interaction of external with internal. Out of this action comes both
romance and significance. The poems are poetic not only in setting but also in theme, imagery, and diction. They often attend to
rhyme and meter. Their chief concern is not with the world of
ordinary men but rather with the world of man, the individual

soul. The one recurrent theme appears to be the efficacy of love and beauty, their power when both are conjoined in overcoming evil. This theme, however, is more often implicit than explicit, for the poems of high imagination are subtly handled. In them, the poet never pontificates, nor does he rely upon the poetry of other eras for materials with which to "stuff" them. If Coleridge borrows the diction of fifteenth-century ballads for the "Ancient Mariner," he does so not to "stuff" but rather to effect the removal of the poem from the ordinary world of men. Thus he brings about in these magical poems that "willing suspension of disbelief" requisite to making each man believe more strongly in his potential for realizing an individual Eden remote from the common world while still capable of ameliorating through individual effort the human condition there existent.

In truth, there are other "Fears in Solitude" than that written by Coleridge and there are other "Frosts at Midnight"; but there are no other "Ancient Mariners" or "Kubla Khans," nor are there likely to be. In evaluating Coleridge's poetry, it can readily be seen and accepted that for the poems of high imagination his reputation is eternally made. For the conversation poems, however, his reputation as thinker, philosopher, and man involved in the contemporary world is currently continually being bolstered. No longer do contemporary critics ignore the conversation poems and attend only to those of high imagination. As George Whalley remarks (and his remark is typical of contemporary criticism), "There are no signs that the three great poems are exhausted, and few signs that anybody is tempted any more to think that these are the only considerable poems Coleridge ever wrote." [2] While Whalley's statement is correct, the fact remains that the magic of the poems of high imagination makes them unique in English poetry.

Attempting to judge Coleridge in his role as dramatist after seeing him in his role as poet is an unhappy task at best. As has been seen, the kind of drama he wrote, while as popular as any in the nineteenth century, was indeed commensurate only with the inferior quality of nineteenth-century drama in general. Although the translation of Schiller's plays is an adequate one, Coleridge's own plays, *Remorse* and *Zapolya,* are merely vehicles for declamatory pronouncements. The characters are hollow; the themes of revenge and remorse, hackneyed. Except for casual references to

Remorse which appear in histories of the drama, his dramas are unknown today. Undoubtedly, work needs to be done in this area, but such work when completed will be of interest only to the most esoteric literary historian.

As literary critic, Coleridge makes his greatest contribution next to that made in his role as poet. Indeed, Coleridge's literary criticism is enjoying today perhaps a greater vogue than are his three greatest poems. There are good and sufficient reasons for this, as a recent issue of the *Times Literary Supplement* points out.[3] Coleridge's particular mode of criticism has been seen to be descriptive and appreciative, rather than minutely analytical. His criticism extends not only to the entire range of English literature, but also to the literature of other countries. Coleridge, as indicated, spent much of his time with two major figures: Shakespeare and Wordsworth. It was his habit to meditate and philosophize about literature rather than to observe it clinically. In fact, because of this contemplative approach, Coleridge, compared with modern critics of today, has held up well. There are few among the moderns who can convey the essence of the work under study with the same degree of enthusiasm and appreciation for the work itself with which Coleridge infects his readers. Coleridge possessed this faculty not only because he thought deeply about the work as a whole, but also because he recognized his audience for what they were and for what they would become as a result of having read the work being criticized. A comment extracted from the *Times Literary Supplement* casts light upon one of the reasons why modern critics fail to achieve what Coleridge in his criticism achieved, that is, the re-creation of the work itself.

In speaking of the modern critic, the article's author has this to say: "He has rarely the general reader in view: a university critic with a gift for crisp writing is likely to have his style described by his colleagues, as his 'rhetoric.' The critic as primarily a man of letters has become almost an extinct animal. . . . Cannot . . . too much emphasis on niggling appreciation of the short passage tend to destroy a young student's omniverousness, his enthusiasm and excitement about how much there is to read?"[4]

As this same writer confirms, Coleridge saw that the function of imagination was to work upon both the poet and upon the reader of his poem.[5] The role of the reader-critic becomes then not only one of analysis and evaluation, but also one of creation. According to this criterion, Coleridge stands in the first rank of critics, for as a critic he was never far removed from himself as a poet. For this reason, he not only wrote *about* literature, as George Steiner says moderns are prone to do exclusively, but he also wrote literature. His vast erudition and his own poetic creativity gave him a distinct advantage over the typical modern critic. Coleridge made ". . . the effort of personal judgment," and yet in making that effort, he chose usually to praise rather than to disparage the work under consideration.[6]

Although there is no place in this study for a chapter on Coleridge's contributions to modern criticism, it is appropriate to mention that almost all modern "schools" are indebted to him for theory. As theoretical critic, that is, one who is more concerned with principles than with practice, Coleridge enjoys their respect. For example, the Neo-Humanists (Bush, More, Babbitt) admire him for the respect he accords to human values. The Neo-Aristotelians (Wimsatt, Crane) respect him for his belief that "first principles" are of the essence. The so-called New Critics (Brooks, Eliot, Warren) have literally taken over his concepts of "organic unity" and the "reconciliation of opposites," emending the latter to mean "tension." There remains a great deal of work still to be done in examining Coleridge's critical theory and literary criticism per se. The contributions of I. A. Richards, George Watson, Herbert Read, and Richard Harter Fogle have been noticed. The task of examining the criticism further will be made somewhat easier, as George Whalley points out, when the complete edition of Coleridge now in progress is finished.[7]

In turning to Coleridge as philosopher, one meets with divided opinion. I. A. Richards makes the statement, "Coleridge was not, I suppose, a good philosopher," [8] while Muirhead, himself an eminent philosopher, undertakes to demonstrate the genius of Coleridge for seizing upon crucial first principles.[9] For most modern students of literature, Coleridge's philosophical writings are pertinent only for the light they throw upon his critical tenets and, in general, upon the method of his criticism. Borrowing now from this one, now from that, fashioning all such grist into his own "metaphysic," Coleridge can scarcely be said to be a systematic philosopher. It must be remembered, however, that his philosophical plan was unfinished. Had there been time, he might well have become more "systematic" than any has yet supposed. Certainly, for the student of Coleridge as poet and as literary critic, an acquaintance with the philosophical writings is essential. The concepts of imagination and fancy are, for example, much more readily understood in conjunction with those of reason and understanding. The converse is similarly true. There remains much to be done, however, with the philosophical writings. This work awaits not only the publication of the complete edition of Coleridge's work, but also the attention of scholars carefully trained in philosophy. One aspect of Coleridge as philosopher, for example, that is seemingly neglected is Coleridge as logician and mathematician.[10]

In conclusion, one of the worst problems confronting Coleridge scholars is undoubtedly the enormous amount of time which even cursory contact with the man demands. For example, for over forty years, Professor Earl Leslie Griggs has been collecting the letters. When the job is finished, which it very nearly is, a new biography will not only be warranted but absolutely necessary.[11] The completion of the *Notebooks* will also be essential to such a study, and it too has kept its editor, Professor Kathleen Coburn, engrossed over a period of many years. In the meantime, certain shibboleths concerning the man and his work must be set aside, for they too raise certain hazards for the scholar. First of all, the concept of Coleridge as an indolent inebriate and drug addict must be tempered. Secondly, the idea of Coleridge as fuzzy-minded, unsystematic, and capricious must be foregone, at least until the availability of all manuscript material shows if such a judgment be true. Based on the material now available, it looks very much as if early estimates of Coleridge still merit acceptance. One estimate was given by John Stuart Mill in 1838, four years after Coleridge's death. Mill was writing at the time on Jeremy Bentham and Coleridge, whom he considered in antithetical ways to be the two most influential minds of the age. He had this to say:

The writers of whom we speak have never been read by the multitude; except for the more slight of their works, their readers have been few: but they have been the teachers of the teachers; there is hardly to be found in England an individual of any importance in the world of mind, who (whatever opinions he may have afterwards adopted) did not first learn to think from these two; and though their influences have but begun to diffuse themselves through these intermediate channels over society at large, there is scarcely a publication of any consequence addressed to the educated classes, which, if these persons had not existed, would not have been different from what it is. These men are, Jeremy Bentham and Samuel Taylor Coleridge—the two great seminal minds of England in their age.[12]

Although Jeremy Bentham may now be relegated to the fields of economics and philosophy, Samuel Taylor Coleridge continues in retrospect to be for today what Mill saw him to be for yesterday: the seminal mind of his age. Nor was Coleridge himself unaware of the properties of his mind, for he stated in the *Biographia* with some humor, "I have laid too many eggs in the hot sands of this wilderness, the world, with ostrich carelessness and ostrich oblivion. The greater part indeed have been trod under foot, and are forgotten; but yet no small number have crept forth into life, some to furnish feathers for the caps of others, and still more to plume the shafts in the quivers of my enemies, of them that unprovoked have lain in wait against my soul."[13] These early estimates by Mill and by Coleridge himself will very likely prove to be, in the final analysis, as comprehensive and as valid as any.

Notes and References

Chapter One

1. Both the day of Coleridge's birth and the number of his brothers and sisters seem to be somewhat in question. Lawrence Hanson, *The Life of S. T. Coleridge* (New York, 1939), gives the day of birth as October 20 and the number of children as fourteen, p. 11; James Dykes Campbell, ed., *The Complete Poetical and Dramatic Works of S. T. Coleridge* (London, 1907), in his authoritative, though early sketch of the life, gives the day of birth as October 21, and the number of children, thirteen, p. xi. Most authorities agree with Campbell. See Ernest Bernbaum, *Guide Through the Romantic Movement* (New York, 1949), p. 53; also, *Dictionary of National Biography* (London, 1922), IV, 758; also Kathleen Raine, *Coleridge* (London, 1958), p. 5. It matters little that these contradictions exist, except to point out that there are many such inconsistencies in Coleridge scholarship. Because almost no date can be regarded "common knowledge," extensive documentation becomes essential.

2. Hanson, p. 12.

3. *Ibid.*

4. Campbell, p. xiii.

5. Charles Lamb, *Essays of Elia* (New York, 1942), pp. 18–19.

6. Earl Leslie Griggs, ed., *The Collected Letters of Samuel Taylor Coleridge* (Oxford, 1956), I, pp. 302–3 to Thomas Poole (February, 1798), Coleridge describes in retrospect the meager fare of the school. Hereafter, Grigg's letters will be cited by the short title, CL, plus appropriate volume number.

7. Lamb, p. 25.

8. Campbell, pp. xv–xvi.

9. Lamb, pp. 19, 22.

10. Lamb, p. 24.

11. Hanson, p. 24.

12. Campbell, pp. xvii, xviii; see also, S. T. Coleridge, *The Biographia Literaria*, ed. J. Shawcross (Oxford, 1907), I, pp. 16–17—hereafter *Biographia*. For more on Bowles, his poetry and his influence, see W. L. Renwick, *English Literature* (Oxford, 1963), pp. 101–2.

13. Campbell, p. xviii.
14. Hanson, p. 29.
15. *Ibid.*, p. 35.
16. Campbell, p. xx.
17. Hanson, p. 41; Campbell, p. xx.
18. CL, I, p. 83.
19. CL, I, p. 103.
20. *Ibid.*
21. Hanson, p. 42.
22. *Ibid.*
23. Campbell, pp. xxvi–xxvii.
24. CL, I, p. 173.
25. Campbell, p. xxvii.
26. Hanson, pp. 75–76.
27. Hanson, p. 75.
28. Campbell, p. xxvii.
29. CL, I, pp. 184–85.
30. CL, I, p. 185.
31. CL, I, p. 184.
32. CL, I, p. 185.
33. Campbell, p. xxix; Hanson, pp. 141–51.
34. Campbell, p. xxx.
35. CL, I, p. 288.
36. The letters abound in descriptions of Coleridge's several maladies. See CL, II, pp. 664–65; 668; 1034–35; 1044–47; 1048–49; *et passim.*
37. Campbell, p. xxx.
38. John E. Jordan, *De Quincey to Wordsworth* (Los Angeles, 1962), especially Chapter V, pp. 334–65.
39. Lucy Gillman Watson, *Coleridge at Highgate* (New York, 1925), p. 19.
40. Elisabeth Schneider, *Coleridge, Opium, and "Kubla Khan"* (Chicago, 1953).
41. Campbell, p. xxxiii.
42. For the dating of poems, see Ernest Hartley Coleridge, ed., *The Complete Poetical Works of Samuel Taylor Coleridge*, 2 vols. (Oxford, 1957)—this edition is based on the first edition of 1912.
43. Amy Cruse, *The Englishman and His Books* (New York, n.p.d.), p. 37.
44. Campbell, p. xv.
45. Cruse, pp. 49–57.
46. Emile Legouis, "Some Remarks on the Composition of the *Lyrical Ballads* of 1798," in *Wordsworth and Coleridge: Studies in Honor of*

George McLean Harper, ed. Earl Leslie Griggs (Princeton, 1939), pp. 1–11.

47. Campbell, pp. xiv–xvii.

48. CL, I, pp. 445–49; 453–54, *et passim.*

49. Campbell, pp. xlvii–xlix.

50. *Ibid.,* pp. lv–lvi.

51. CL, I, letter to Daniel Stuart (March, 1800), p. 581; and to Poole (July, 1800), p. 607.

52. CL, I, pp. 619, 635, 656.

53. CL, I, p. 608.

54. Campbell, p. lxvi.

55. CL, II, pp. 616–66 contain some of the most detailed accounts of Coleridge's specific afflictions; see also, pp. 868–69, 875, 902–3, *et passim.*

56. Campbell, pp. lxix–lxx.

57. *Ibid.,* p. lxxi.

58. *Ibid.,* pp. lxxv–lxxx.

59. CL, III, pp. 336–38; in Griggs, *Unpublished Letters of Samuel Taylor Coleridge* (New Haven, 1933), II, p. 58, the sentence reads, "Would to heaven the same thing was true of the Wordsworth family towards me." This sentence is not given in CL, III; evidently Professor Griggs became more cautious in this latter interpolation, for CL, III, p. 338, reads "several words inked out in manuscript."

60. Griggs, *Unpublished Letters* . . . , II, p. 104.

61. CL, III, pp. 476–77.

62. CL, III, p. 491.

63. Campbell, pp. lxxiv–xcvi.

64. See Alice D. Snyder, *Coleridge on Logic and Learning* (New Haven, 1929), for a description of these fragments.

65. Cf. notes 38–40 above; see also Campbell, who states that by 1814 Coleridge's consumption of laudanum had reached two quarts per week and at times as much as one pint per day, p. xci.

66. CL, III, p. 477.

67. *Biographia,* I, p. 9.

68. James V. Baker, *The Sacred River* (Baton Rouge, 1957), pp. 16–19.

69. Arthur O. Lovejoy, "Coleridge and Kant's Two Worlds," in *Essays in the History of Ideas* (New York, 1960)—Lovejoy makes the point that Kant's philosophy is also in actuality opposed to that ultimately evolved by Coleridge, pp. 259–60.

70. Baker, pp. 14–16; 19–20.

71. Baker, p. 21.

72. *Biographia,* I, pp. 92–93.

73. *Ibid.*, p. 98.
74. *Ibid.*
75. *Biographia*, I, p. 133; see also Shedd, ed., *The Complete Works of Samuel Taylor Coleridge* (New York, 1853), I, p. 211; VI, pp. 301–2.
76. *Biographia*, I, p. 102.
77. Shedd, *Works*, I, p. 23, for a discussion of Coleridge's borrowing of the doctrine of Subject and Object.
78. Shedd, *Works*, I, pp. 25–33, on Kant's influence; see also Lovejoy, *Essays . . .* , pp. 254–76; and further, John Muirhead, *Coleridge As Philosopher* (New York, 1954), pp. 52–59.
79. Campbell, pp. xcvi–cvi.
80. *Ibid.*
81. *Ibid.*, pp. cvi–cxi.
82. Lucy Watson, pp. 60–65; see also the full treatment of this subject in Richard Armour and Raymond Howes, eds., *Coleridge the Talker* (Ithaca, 1940).
83. Campbell, pp. cx–cxi.
84. Lucy Watson, p. 83.
85. *Ibid.*, p. 96.
86. Campbell, pp. cxiv–cxix; see also D. G. James, *The Romantic Comedy* (New York, 1948), pp. 161–62, for a more fully developed account of Coleridge's religious progress.
87. Lucy Watson, pp. 158–59.
88. Campbell, pp. cxxi–cxxii.

Chapter Two

1. Writing about Romanticism and Romantics, like writing about Coleridge himself, can turn into one long and complex qualification. For this reason, the more specialized student is urged to consult the many excellent essays now readily available in Robert F. Gleckner and Gerald E. Enscoe, eds., *Romanticism: Points of View* (Englewood Cliffs, New Jersey, 1962). This compact volume contains many of the classic and modern statements on the subject. Essays by Grierson, Bernbaum, Fogle, and Peckham are among the most helpful to the beginning student; essays by Babbitt, Brooks, Lovejoy, Lucas, and Wellek are helpful to those who already have a grasp of Romanticism as traditionally conceived.
2. See Gleckner and Enscoe, essays by Lovejoy, Hulme, and Fairchild, which in part tend to wipe out Romanticism as traditionally conceived; essays by Babbitt, Brooks, Lucas, and Wellek are unsympathetic to Romanticism per se though in varying degrees.
3. There is no pat definition of Romanticism. There are many definitions. Too many of them seem to indicate that their authors have not

read the Romantics for some time before attempting definition. To my way of thinking, Bernbaum's general discussion in *Guide through the Romantic Movement* (Revised edition, 1949), is still the best general discussion; he lists some twenty-nine definitions, their sources, pp. 301–2, and above all he is clear.

4. Professor C. M. Bowra, *The Romantic Imagination* (Cambridge, Mass., 1949), has the best discussion of the creative process as the Romantics conceived of it. Bowra, interestingly, is not a Romantic but rather a classical "specialist." See p. 1 *et passim.*

5. Ernest Lee Tuveson, *The Imagination As a Means of Grace* (Berkeley, 1960), while not sympathetic to the concept of the Romantic imagination as a kind of "mystique," lucidly discusses the sources of the concept. See particularly, p. 17.

6. When the Imagination looks to the world of the understanding for its materials, it may be said to be working with the *natural* supernatural. When the Imagination turns in upon itself and seeks to create out of the irrational, un-ordered, or chaotic, it may be said to be working with the *supernatural* supernatural. William Wordsworth provides his readers with examples of the former, the *natural* supernatural, in action. For example, he uses daisies, celandines, daffodils; he uses uncorrupted little girls, such as Lucy and the child in "We Are Seven"; he uses simple rural people, such as Michael, the leech-gatherer, the Highland girl. He uses all of these natural objects, so to speak, in order to effect a recognition of the *spiritual*—and in this sense, of course, the spiritual is the supernatural. Coleridge uses the same technique in the "conversation poems." Sarah Fricker Coleridge is the pure in heart of "The Eolian Harp," while Sara Hutchinson is the uncorrupted of "Dejection: An Ode." Both "Frost At Midnight" and "This Lime-tree Bower" use the natural in order to effect the supernatural (spiritual). But Coleridge in the poems of high imagination uses a different technique or mode of approach. Here he uses the *supernatural* supernatural; that is, he removes his subjects from the realm of ordinary or common sense. He selects a witch-like Geraldine in "Christabel," a mesmeric empowered old mariner in "The Ancient Mariner," a land remote from any that is familiar in "Kubla Khan." In summary, then, the natural supernatural finds its impetus in the world of the common sense while the supernatural supernatural finds its impetus and its realization in the world of the un-common sense.

7. Mario Praz, *The Romantic Agony* (London, 1933), discusses the frenetic, bizarre, and more moribund aspects of this world of the un-common sense to which certain Romantics in certain poems were directed.

8. The discussion here is not wholly fair to the eighteenth-century neo-classicists, but is an attempt through exaggeration to point up their

consolidated position in order to juxtapose it with the Romantic point of view. As Hulme points out, the distinction is never thus sharply and singly antithetical. See Hulme, "Romanticism and Classicism," in Gleckner and Enscoe, pp. 34–44.

9. For a discussion of these terms, see Chapters VIII and IX this study.

10. *Biographia,* II, p. 187.

Chapter Three

1. All references to Coleridge's poems are from *The Complete Works* . . . , edited by E. H. Coleridge, 2 vols. (London, 1912; revised edition 1957)—hereafter, *Poems,* I, or *Poems,* II, and appropriate page. All dates of poems are taken from this edition. Where the date of composition differs from the date of publication, both are given in that order within parentheses in the text.

2. *Poems,* I, potpourri in order of appearance in the text, pp. 8–9, 56, 21–24, 74–76, 18–19, 17–18, 17, 34, 19–20, 59–63, 70 *et passim,* 11–12.

3. *Poems,* I, pp. 49–50.

4. *Poems,* I, pp. 51–54; hereafter, references given in text by appropriate lines only.

5. All references to Wordsworth's poems are from *The Complete Works of William Wordsworth,* ed. A. J. George (Boston: Houghton Mifflin, 1932).

6. *Poems,* I, pp.79–90.

7. *Poems,* I, p. 84, ll. 13–14.

8. *Poems,* I, pp. 13–15.

9. *Poems,* I, pp. 125–31.

10. *Poems,* I, "The Destiny of Nations," pp. 131–48.

11. *Poems,* I, "Ode to a Departing Year," pp. 160–68.

12. *Ibid.,* ll. 13–35; cf. also note 1, p. 161.

13. *Poems,* I, pp. 108–25.

Chapter Four

1. Archibald MacLeish, "Ars poetica," in *Poems, 1924–1933* (New York, 1933), pp. 122–23.

2. *Poems,* I, pp. 100–2; hereafter references cited by appropriate lines given in parentheses within text itself.

3. "Tension" in this study is taken to mean any stress created by the existence of opposite entities, qualities, images, etc. Not to be confused with "tension" as discussed by John Crowe Ransom in *The New Criticism* (Norfolk, Conn., 1941), p. 295; also see, Sylvan Barnet, Morton Berman, William Burto, *The Study of Literature* (Boston, 1960), pp. 303–5, for a capsule review of the term's more specialized meaning.

4. *Poems,* I, pp. 106–8; hereafter by appropriate lines in text itself.
5. *Poems,* I, pp. 178–81.
6. *Poems,* I, cf. footnote 1, p. 181.
7. *Poems,* I, pp. 243–47.
8. *Poems,* I, pp. 256–63.
9. *Poems,* I, p. 257.
10. *Poems,* I, pp. 240–42.

Chapter Five

"The Rime of the Ancient Mariner"

1. Harold Bloom, *The Visionary Company* (New York, 1961)—uses this term to stand for that quality which I have chosen to call "High Imagination." That is, that which differentiates the major poems from the conversation poems treated in the preceding chapter.
2. *Poems,* I, pp. 186–209; hereafter by lines within parentheses within the text.
3. Cf. Chapter VIII, for a full explication of Coleridge's concept of Imagination and Fancy, parallelled in Chapter IX by a discussion of his distinction between Reason and Understanding. At the time of the writing of the poems of High Imagination, Coleridge had not yet recorded this distinction though he may well have already conceived of it.
4. *Poems,* I, p. 194; this information is revealed specifically in the marginal gloss; the appropriate lines merely imply this.
5. *Ibid.,* p. 201.

"Christabel"

6. *Poems,* I, pp. 213–36; the gist of the comments here appear in my article, *"Christabel:* Directions Old and New," *Studies in English Literature* (October, 1964).
7. Arthur Nethercot, *The Road to Tryermaine* (Chicago, 1939), pp. 4–12; John Livingston Lowes, *The Road to Xanadu* (Boston, 1927).
8. Kathleen Coburn, ed., *The Notebooks of Samuel Taylor Coleridge* (New York, 1947), I, pp. 940, 942, 1000, 1063—hereafter cited as *Notebooks.*
9. Roy P. Basler, *Sex Symbolism and Psychology* (New Brunswick, 1948), pp. 3–51; and Edgar Jones, "A New Reading of *Christabel,"* *The Cambridge Journal,* V (November, 1951–1952), 97–110.
10. *Poems,* I, pp. 213–36, cf. both text of poem and "machinery" appropriate to it.
11. *Poems,* I, note on page 224; the incident in which Shelley ran from the room is recounted in Leslie Marchand, *Byron* (New York, 1957), II, pp. 629–30.
12. *Poems,* I, p. 224; notes to "Christabel."
13. For an account of Coleridge's plan to complete "Christabel," cf.

James Gillman, *Life of Samuel Taylor Coleridge* (London, 1838), I, pp. 301–2; this account would support the "witch" reading, but the poem as we have it seems to uphold the psychological reading.

14. Nethercot, p. 35; see also E. H. Coleridge note on "The Ballad of the Dark Ladie," in *Poems*, I, p. 293.

15. Richard Harter Fogle, *The Idea of Coleridge's Criticism* (Los Angeles: Univ. of Cal. Press, 1962), contains a very interesting essay on "Christabel" which attempts to illuminate the poem by applying Coleridge's own principles of criticism, namely that of the reconciliation of opposites. I myself have followed this method of criticism in some of the other poems, but feel that "Christabel" is more important for its treatment of ambivalent love relationships than as a model of Coleridgean criticism per se.

"Kubla Khan"

16. *Poems*, I; see Coleridge's introductory statement cited in this text, pp. 295–96. Full text of the poem, pp. 295–98.

17. *Ibid.*

18. Numerous articles exist in support of this statement. For example, see, Elisabeth Schneider, "The 'Dream' of 'Kubla Khan.' " *PMLA*, LX (September, 1945), 784–801; see also, N. B. Allen, "A Note on Coleridge's 'Kubla Khan,' " *Modern Language Notes*, LVII (February, 1942), 108–13.

19. For the distinction between Coleridge's concept of the Imagination and that of the Understanding see, respectively, pp. 128–30; 152–53, this study.

20. For the "secondary imagination" and its function, see p. 129, this study.

21. Cf. *Biographia Literaria*, II, p. 6.

"The Ballad of the Dark Ladie" and "Lewti"

22. *Poems*, I, "Love," pp. 330–35.

23. *Ibid.*, "The Ballad of the Dark Ladie," pp. 293–95.

24. *Ibid.*, see Ernest Hartley Coleridge's note to the poem, p. 293.

25. *Ibid.*, "Lewti," pp. 253–56.

Chapter Six

1. *Poems*, I, "Hymn Before Sunrise," pp. 376–80; see note 2 below text of poem.

2. See letter to Southey, September 11, 1803, in Griggs, CL, II, pp. 982–84.

3. *Poems*, I, "The Pains of Sleep," pp. 389-91, here quoted ll. 1–13.

4. *Poems*, I, "Dejection: An Ode," pp. 362–68.

5. CL, II, pp. 813–19.

6. *Poems*, I, see note 2, pp. 362–63.

7. CL, II, p. 814.

8. *Ibid.*, pp. 814–15.

9. William Wordsworth, *The Complete Works of William Words-worth*, edited by A. J. George (Cambridge, Mass., 1932), p. 281; ll. 48–49—hereafter, *Works*.

10. *Ibid.*, p. 92; ll. 104–11.

11. Letter to Sotheby, July 19, 1802, in Griggs, CL, II, p. 814.

12. *Ibid.*

13. The line beginning, "O Lady . . ." was first given as "O Edmund." Coleridge wished to hide his love for Sara Hutchinson from the world. See textual emendations in footnotes, *Poems*, I, pp. 364–65.

14. *Works*, p. 326; ll. 14–16.

Chapter Seven

1. A. W. Ward, ed., *Cambridge History of English Literature* (New York, 1914), II, p. 285—hereafter by short title, *CHEL*.

2. Allardyce Nicoll, *A History of Early Nineteenth Century Drama* (Cambridge, 1930), I, pp. 58–59.

3. *Ibid.*, Chapter V.

4. *Ibid.*, I, p. 192.

5. *Ibid.*, I, p. 193.

6. *Ibid.*, pp. 65–66.

7. *Ibid.*, p. 62; see also E. Bradlee Watson, *Sheridan to Robertson: A Study of the Nineteenth-Century London Stage* (Cambridge, Mass., 1926), pp. 136–39.

8. Nicoll, I, pp. 7–9; 61–63. Another problem to be faced was the paucity of numbers of theaters and also the inconvenience to those few theaters that enjoyed sanction of rigorous court control. Theaters fell into two categories: "legitimate" and "illegitimate." Those in the former were licensed by the court. Until the Theater Act of 1848, there were but two of these latter, Drury Lane and Covent Garden. Both were huge halls with bad acoustics. Both also were subject to the restrictions of the court. This meant that the court censors decided what plays were appropriate for production and what plays were not. Theaters that were not licensed by the court had to prove that they were "variety" theaters if they were to be allowed to remain open. These interspersed animal acts, jugglers, ballet, song and dance routines, between acts of serious drama. By so doing, they avoided being closed by the Lord Chancellor, I, pp. 7–47; see also *CHEL*, XIII (no. II), pp. 283–85.

9. For information concerning publication dates, production dates, place where produced, etc., see Nicoll, II, which contains a list of such information.

10. Material is not readily available on Coleridge as dramatist. It is interesting to note that David Daiches, *A Critical History of English Literature* (New York, 1960), II, pp. 888–902, makes no mention whatsoever of Coleridge as dramatist. George Pierce Baker in Watson, *Sheridan to Robertson,* speaks as follows: "Knowledge of English drama from 1800–1900 has been much like our knowledge of central Africa in the seventies of the nineteenth century." p. i, preface.

11. *Poems,* II, pp. 495–517; hereafter by act, scene, and lines only, references given in parentheses within text of study itself.

12. For more on Coleridge as political philosopher, see his own remarks in *Conciones ad populum, The Watchman* (1795–1796), *The Friend* (1809–10; 1818), *The Constitution of Church and State* (1830); see also Carl R. Woodring, *Politics in the Poetry of Coleridge* (Madison, 1961); and *CHEL,* XI, pp. 153–54.

13. *Poems,* II, pp. 598–811, inclusive for the text of both *The Piccolomini* and *The Death of Wallenstein.* It is easy to see why Coleridge selected Schiller as worthy of translation. Not only for the poetry per se, but also for Schiller's passionate love of freedom and for his devotion to idealism was he a poet worthy of Coleridge's attention. Coleridge remained faithful for the most part to the original text of Schiller's plays. He did not of course translate the Largo of the original trilogy, and he did take some liberties with superficial aspects of the plays. For example, he lengthened *The Piccolomini* but only by extending it to cover Acts I and II of the original *Death of Wallenstein.* In the latter play, he did some rearranging of scenes, notably minor scenes in the last part of the play. Cf. Act III of Coleridge's translation is Act IV of Schiller's play. To hear the German lines of the Schiller, however, is to hear a smoothness and beauty not truly approximated in the translation.

14. Allardyce Nicoll, *A History of Late Eighteenth Century Drama, 1750–1800* (Cambridge, Mass., 1937), p. 245; for facts surrounding, see also *Poems,* II, p. 819.

15. Excerpts from these reviews are readily available in S. T. Coleridge, *Osorio* (London, 1873), see monograph by publisher, John Pearson, pp. i–xxii.

16. Discussion based on text, *Poems,* II, pp. 812–83—hereafter references given to act, scene, lines, within text itself in parentheses this study.

17. Letter to John Rickman, January 25, 1813, in Griggs, CL, III, p. 428.

18. CL, III, pp. 433–34.
19. *Ibid.*
20. CL, IV, p. 563.
21. *Poems,* II, text of *Zapolya,* pp. 883–950.
22. *Ibid.*, p. 883.
23. *Ibid.*
24. CL, IV, p. 588.
25. Letter to John Murry, February 27, 1817, CL, IV, pp. 703–7.

Chapter Eight

1. I. A. Richards, *Coleridge on Imagination* (London, 1934).
2. Richard Harter Fogle, *The Idea of Coleridge's Criticism* (Los Angeles, 1962).
3. Kathleen Coburn, *Notebooks of Samuel Taylor Coleridge,* 2 vols. (New York, 1957–   ).
4. Walter Jackson Bate, *Prefaces to Criticism* (New York, 1959), p. 154; and currently in preparation, *The Complete Works of Coleridge* in twenty-seven volumes, cf. reference to this in George Whalley, "Coleridge Unlabyrinthed," *The University of Toronto Quarterly,* XXXII (July, 1963), p. 326.
5. George Watson, *The Literary Critics* (London, 1962), pp. 13–14.
6. See letter regarding every man either an Aristotelian or a Platonist in Griggs, *Unpublished Letters of Samuel Taylor Coleridge,* Letter to J. Gooden, January 14, [1820] (New Haven, 1933), II, pp. 264–66.
7. Elliott Coleman, ed., *Lectures in Criticism* (New York, 1961)—introduction by Huntington Cairns, p. 1.
8. Bate, pp. 99–122; see also pp. 3–22.
9. George Watson, pp. 111–12.
10. Samuel Taylor Coleridge, *Biographia Literaria,* ed. J. Shawcross (Oxford, 1907), I, p. xcii—hereafter, *Biographia.*
11. George Watson, p. 117; *Biographia,* I, p. xcii.
12. *Biographia,* I, pp. xciv–xcv.
13. Fogle, pp. x–xiv; pp. 7–10; see also M. H. Abrams, *The Mirror and the Lamp* (New York, 1958), pp. 167–77—for an excellent discussion of Coleridge's concept of organic unity, which Abrams terms "organic imagination."
14. Fogle, p. 10.
15. Baker, *The Sacred River* (Baton Rouge, 1959), p. 267.
16. *Biographia,* I, p. 109.
17. *Ibid.*, II, p. 10.
18. *Ibid.*, p. 11.
19. George Watson, pp. 112–15.

20. George Watson, p. 130; see also discussion of this point by Herbert Read, "Coleridge As Critic," in *Lectures in Criticism,* ed. Elliot Coleman, pp. 88–90.

21. *Biographia,* I, p. 202.

22. Fogle, p. 7.

23. *Biographia,* I, p. 202.

24. *Ibid.*

25. *Ibid.*

26. *Ibid.*

27. See Bate, *Prefaces to Criticism,* pp. 115–16, for a discussion of "organic" in Coleridge's conception and "organic" in the modern critical spectrum.

28. *Biographia,* I, p. 107.

29. See commentary on *Romeo and Juliet,* pp. 143–44 this study.

30. *Biographia,* I, p. 62.

31. *Ibid.,* pp. 21–23.

32. *Ibid.,* p. 14.

33. *Ibid.,* pp. 14–15.

34. *Ibid.,* p. 16.

35. *Ibid.,* p. 15.

36. *Ibid.,* p. 44.

37. Such a statement may well be apocryphal, for the influence upon Wordsworth by Coleridge and Coleridge by Wordsworth has been greatly debated both pro and con.

38. *Biographia,* I, pp. 56–60.

39. *Ibid.,* p. 59.

40. *Ibid.,* p. 51.

41. George Watson, pp. 114–15.

42. *Biographia,* I, pp. 50–52.

43. *Biographia,* II, p. 6.

44. *Ibid.*

45. *Biographia,* I, p. 64.

46. *Ibid.*

47. From the "Preface to the *Lyrical Ballads*" in *The Complete Works of William Wordsworth,* ed. Andrew George (Cambridge, 1932), p. 791; for other objections see comment on Wordsworth's use of dialogue in Shedd, *Table Talk,* VI, p. 403.

48. *Biographia,* II, p. 42, p. 45.

49. *Ibid.,* pp. 77–85.

50. *Ibid.,* p. 80.

51. *Ibid.,* pp. 97–109.

52. *Ibid.,* pp. 115–24.

53. *Ibid.,* p. 124.

54. See Fogle, pp. 70–104, for elaboration on this point.

55. Samuel Taylor Coleridge, *The Friend,* in Shedd, *The Complete Works of* . . . (New York, 1853), II, pp. 408–17.

56. Thomas M. Raysor, ed., *Coleridge's Shakespearian Criticism* (Cambridge, 1930), volume I, which contains the poet's own notes on Shakespeare's poetry and plays; and volume II, which contains Collier's report made after hearing Coleridge's actual lectures on the plays.

57. Samuel Johnson, "Preface to Shakespeare," in *The Works of Samuel Johnson,* ed. Arthur Murphy (London, 1825), pp. 326–44.

58. *Ibid.,* pp. 327–28.

59. *Ibid.,* p. 332.

60. *Ibid.,* pp. 343–44.

61. *Ibid.,* p. 331.

62. *Ibid.,* p. 334.

63. *Ibid.*

64. Raysor points out that there were liberal critics in the eighteenth century (vol. I, p. xxiv) just as there were conservative critics in the nineteenth century. But in general, neo-classic criticism prevailed in the eighteenth century while Romantic prevailed in the nineteenth. Coleridge makes the point in the notebooks that the critic knows a priori that a work must have "defects" and that therefore it comes as no surprise to a reader that this is so. Not all works, however, have "beauties." For this reason, the task of the critic is to search for what may or may not be contained in the work, *Anima Poetae,* ed. Ernest Hartley Coleridge (London, 1895), p. 30.

65. Raysor has a good discussion on the German influences (p. xvii), as does Shawcross also in the introduction to the *Biographia,* I, pp. xi–xcvii.

66. Raysor, I, p. 18; for additional remarks on Hamlet see Shedd, *Table Talk,* in *Works,* VI, p. 285.

67. Raysor, p. 25.

68. *Ibid.,* p. 35; see also Raysor, II, pp. 192–98.

69. Raysor, I, p. 37.

70. *Ibid.,* pp. 38–39.

71. *Ibid.,* p. 39.

72. Raysor, II, p. 194.

73. *Ibid.,* p. 195.

74. Raysor, I, pp. 37–40.

75. Raysor, II, pp. 192–98.

76. George Watson, p. 124.

77. Fogle, pp. 27–28.

78. Shedd, *Works,* vol. II, p. 416.

79. Bate, p. 156.

80. Raysor, I, p. 59.

81. *Ibid.,* p. 78.

82. *Ibid.*

83. Raysor, quoting from *Bristol Gazette,* II, pp. 262–72.

84. *Ibid.,* p. 275.

85. Raysor, I, pp. 77–79.

86. *Ibid.,* p. 54.

87. *Ibid.*

88. *Ibid.,* p. 49.

89. Raysor, "Collier Report," II, p. 127.

90. *Ibid.,* pp. 128–29.

91. *Ibid.,* p. 132; see also Raysor, I, p. 8.

92. Raysor, I, pp. 133–34.

93. Raysor, II, p. 142; see also Raysor, I, pp. 6–7.

94. *Ibid.,* II, p. 144.

95. *Ibid.,* II, p. 192.

96. Raysor, I, p. 155; see also II, pp. 186–88.

97. Raysor, I, 128–30; see also Raysor, I, "Dramatic Illusion," pp. 200–3, *et passim;* see also Raysor, II, pp. 169–81 on discussion of *The Tempest* as an example of an "ideal" play. Further discussions of dramatic illusion and Coleridge's specific concept of it in Fogle, pp. 112–24 and Bate, pp. 155–60.

98. Raysor, I, p. 131.

99. *Ibid.,* I, p. 133.

100. *Biographia,* II, p. 19.

101. Raysor, I, pp. 212–13; see also *Table Talk* in Shedd, *Works,* VI, p. 312, *et passim.*

102. Raysor, I, p. 212.

103. *Ibid.,* p. 214, p. 216.

104. *Ibid.,* p. 212.

105. *Ibid.,* p. 229.

106. *Biographia,* I, p. 48.

107. *Ibid.,* pp. 11–13.

108. Raysor, II, p. 174.

109. *Ibid.,* p. 34.

110. *Ibid.,* p. 39.

111. *Ibid.*

112. *Ibid.,* p. 135.

113. In order of appearance in the text, Donne, in *Biographia,* I, p. 15; Richardson, in Raysor, II, pp. 18–19; Voltaire, Ariosto, and Tasso in Raysor, II, p. 39; Campbell in Raysor, II, p. 44; for rambling notes on various other poets and dramatists, see Mrs. H. N. Coleridge's collection, *Literary Remains,* in Shedd, *Works,* IV. This collection is still supplementary to Raysor as is also *Literary Remains,* edited by Henry Nelson Coleridge, in *Works,* V, which takes up, among

others, Donne, More, Skelton, Robinson, but emphasizes Coleridge's interest in the religious aspect of their writings.

Chapter Nine

1. Alice Snyder, *Coleridge on Logic and Learning* (New Haven, 1929), pp. 12–13.

2. *Biographia*, I, p. 174.

3. *Ibid.*, p. 175.

4. *Ibid.*, p. 179.

5. *Ibid.*

6. Shedd, ed., *Works*, "Table Talk," VI, p. 313—hereafter *Table Talk*.

7. Shedd, *Works*, "Aids to Reflection," I.—hereafter *Aids*.

8. *Ibid.*, pp. 241–42; the debt to Kant's distinction between the "pure" and "practical" reason has been vigorously debated by scholars.

9. *Ibid.*, p. 241.

10. *Ibid.*, p. 242.

11. *Ibid.*, p. 151.

12. *Ibid.*, p. 139.

13. *Ibid.*, p. 242.

14. *Ibid.*, pp. 243–45.

15. *Ibid.*, p. 242.

16. *Ibid.*, p. 246.

17. *Table Talk*, VI, p. 319.

18. Fogle, *The Idea of Coleridge's Criticism*, p. 7.

19. Shedd, *Works*, "Hints Toward the Formation of a more Comprehensive Theory of Life," I, pp. 373–416—hereafter, "Theory of Life."

20. *Ibid.*, p. 383.

21. *Ibid.*, p. 387.

22. *Ibid.*, p. 391.

23. *Ibid.*, p. 390.

24. *Ibid.*, p. 392.

25. *Ibid.*, p. 416.

26. *Aids*, p. 113.

27. *Ibid.*, p. 114.

28. *Ibid.*, p. 128.

29. *Ibid.*, p. 133.

30. *Ibid.*, pp. 133–34.

31. *Ibid.*, p. 134.

32. *Aids*, p. 152.

33. *Ibid.*, p. 193.

34. *Ibid.*

35. *Ibid.*, p. 197.
36. *Table Talk,* p. 230.
37. *Ibid.*, pp. 233–37.
38. *Ibid.*, p. 373.
39. For more on this unfinished work, see Snyder, *Coleridge on Logic and Learning,* pp. 8–11.
40. Ernest Hartley Coleridge, ed., *Anima Poetae* (London, 1895), pp. 104–5; 120–29.
41. *Ibid.*, p. 77.
42. *Ibid.*, pp. 245–56.
43. Lucy Gillman Watson, *Coleridge at Highgate* (New York, 1925), p. 46; and Shedd, *Works,* "Lay Sermons," VI, p. 145. These two authorities seem to be in disagreement regarding publication dates. Shedd attributes both "Lay Sermons" to 1817 and apparently confuses the title page. She is more likely correct in the 1816 and 1817 dates cited.
44. Shedd, *Works,* "Lay Sermons," p. 150—hereafter *Lay Sermons.*
45. *Ibid.*, p. 147.
46. *Ibid.*, p. 184.
47. *Ibid.*, pp. 183–84.
48. *Ibid.*, pp. 182–87.
49. *Ibid.*, pp. 186–87.
50. *Ibid.*, p. 203.
51. *Ibid.*, p. 224.
52. Shedd, *Works,* "The Statesman's Manuel," I, pp. 417–51—hereafter, *Manuel.*
53. *Ibid.*, pp. 421–51.
54. *Ibid.*, p. 428.
55. *Ibid.*, p. 430.
56. *Ibid.*, p. 429.
57. Shedd, *Works,* "The Friend," II, p. 525—hereafter, *The Friend.*
58. *Ibid.*
59. *Ibid.*, p. vii.
60. *Ibid.*
61. *Ibid.*, p. 384.
62. *Ibid.*
63. *Ibid.*, pp. 384–85.
64. *Ibid.*, p. 385.
65. *Ibid.*, p. 386.
66. *Ibid.*, p. 385.
67. *Ibid.*
68. *Ibid.*, pp. vii–viii.
69. *Ibid.*, p. 410.
70. *Ibid.*, p. 414.

71. *Ibid.*, p. 409.
72. *Ibid.*, p. 449.
73. *Ibid.*, pp. 418–19.
74. *Ibid.*, p. 418.
75. *Ibid.*, pp. 418–19.
76. *Ibid.*, p. 422.
77. *Ibid.*, pp. 419–20.
78. *Ibid.*, p. 429.
79. *Ibid.*, p. 462.
80. *Ibid.*
81. *Ibid.*, p. 470.
82. *Ibid.*, p. 458.
83. *Ibid.*
84. *Lay Sermons*, VI, p. 196.

Chapter Ten

1. Harold Bloom, *The Visionary Company* (New York, 1961), pp. 201–15.
2. Whalley, "Coleridge Unlabyrinthed," *The University of Toronto Quarterly*, XXXII (July, 1963), p. 339.
3. *The Times Literary Supplement* (Friday, July 26, 1963).
4. "The Critical Moment," TLS, p. 535.
5. *Ibid.*
6. See Steiner statement in TLS, p. 539.
7. Whalley, pp. 326, 339; the collected works of Coleridge are in preparation under the general editorship of Kathleen Coburn.
8. Richards, *Coleridge on Imagination* (London, 1934), p. 10.
9. Muirhead, *Coleridge As Philosopher* (New York, 1930), p. 259.
10. Snyder, *Coleridge On Logic and Learning*, alludes to Coleridge in these roles.
11. Whalley, p. 326.
12. John Stuart Mill, *On Bentham and Coleridge*, introduction by F. R. Leavis (New York, 1950), pp. 39–41.
13. *Biographia*, I, p. 32.

Selected Bibliography

Working Bibliography: books and articles used in the foregoing study are broken into two categories, primary and secondary.

Primary Sources

Coleridge, Samuel Taylor. *The Complete Poetical Works of Samuel Taylor Coleridge*, ed., Ernest Hartley Coleridge (1912). 2 vols. Oxford: Clarendon Press, 1957. The standard edition composed of volume 1 poetry and volume 2 poetry and dramatic works. Useful to general reader although the following edition is more complete. Present edition contains variant m.s. readings.

————. *The Complete Works of Samuel Taylor Coleridge*, ed., Shedd. 7 volumes. New York: Harper and Bros., 1853. Still the only edition close to "complete." Will be superseded by the Kathleen Coburn edition when it becomes available.

————. *The Complete Poetical and Dramatic Works of Samuel Taylor Coleridge*, ed., with a biographical introduction by James Dykes Campbell. London: Macmillan, 1907. pp. xi–cxxiv useful biographical material is unsurpassed by later biographies.

————. *Unpublished Letters of Samuel Taylor Coleridge*, ed., Earl Leslie Griggs. 2 vols. New Haven: Yale University Press, 1933. In many ways a more imaginative through perhaps less useful edition of the letters now superseded by the following.

————. *Collected Letters of Samuel Taylor Coleridge*, ed., Earl Leslie Griggs. 4 vols. Oxford: Clarendon Press, 1956. When complete, will make a new biography based on the letters essential.

————. *Anima Poetae*, ed., Ernest Hartley Coleridge. London: William Heinemann, 1895. Collection from the then unpublished Notebooks of STC. Remains the best edition of samples from them. For the full text of the Notebooks, see Kathleen Coburn, ed., *Notebooks of STC*, in progress.

————. *Biographia Literaria*, ed., J. Shawcross. 2 vols. Oxford: Clarendon Press, 1907. The best edition of this important Coleridge work.

————. *Coleridge's Shakespearian Criticism*, ed., Thomas Middleton

Raysor. 2 vols. Cambridge: Harvard University Press, 1930. Still the best edition of the Shakespearian criticism with a long and useful introduction by the editor.

————. *Notebooks of Samuel Taylor Coleridge,* ed., Kathleen Coburn. 2 vols. New York: Pantheon Books, 1957– . Still to be completed. These volumes, each with its companion volume of notes to the notes, are rich in source materials for the more specialized scholar.

————. *Osorio.* London: John Pearson, 1873. Contains a useful monograph by the publishers which acknowledges a debt to Derwent Coleridge for helpful suggestions. Also contains contemporary newspaper reviews of Coleridge's play, *Remorse.*

Miscellaneous Primary

The Works of Samuel Johnson, ed., Arthur Murphy. 2 vols. London: Jones and Company, 1825.

Lamb, Charles. *Essays of Elia.* New York: E. P. Dutton, 1942.

MacLeish, Archibald. *Poems,* 1924–1933. "Ars poetica." New York: Houghton Mifflin, 1933, pp. 122–23.

Wordsworth, William. *The Complete Works of William Wordsworth,* ed., Andrew J. George. Boston: Houghton Mifflin Co., 1932.

Secondary Sources

Abrams, M. H. *The Mirror and the Lamp.* New York: Norton, 1958. Excellent for theory of Romantic poetry.

Allen, N. B. "A Note on Coleridge's 'Kubla Khan,'" *Modern Language Notes,* LVII (February, 1942), 108–13. An attempt to ascertain the extent of opium addiction on the writing of the poem.

Armour, Richard W. and Raymond F. Howes. *Coleridge the Talker.* Ithaca: Cornell University Press, 1940. Another aspect of the myriad-minded STC. Here the brilliant and discursive talker.

Baker, James Volant. *The Sacred River: Coleridge's Theory of the Imagination.* Baton Rouge: Louisiana State University Press, 1957. Interesting in its discussion of the extent to which the process is conscious versus unconscious.

Barnet, Sylvan, Morton Berman, and William Burto. *The Study of Literature.* Boston: Little Brown, 1960. See for capsule review of meaning of "tension."

Basler, Roy P. *Sex, Symbolism, and Psychology in Literature.* New Brunswick: Rutgers University Press, 1948. Essay on "Christabel" interprets that poem from a psychosexual point of view.

Bate, Walter Jackson. *Prefaces to Criticism.* New York: Doubleday Anchor Books, 1959. Breaks criticism into Classical and Romantic traditions. Very good on the former.

Selected Bibliography

Bernbaum, Ernest. *Guide Through the Romantic Movement.* New York: The Ronald Press, 1949. One of the most useful and informative of the introductory books. Selective, but excellent, bibliographies. Compact essays on the pre-Romantics, Romantics, and on the general characteristics of the period.

Bloom, Harold. *The Visionary Company.* New York: Doubleday, 1961. Sub-titled, "A reading of English Romantic Poetry," but not as well supported as one might wish.

Bowra, C. M. *The Romantic Imagination.* Cambridge, Mass.: Harvard University Press, 1949. Although Professor Bowra is a Classics' scholar, this essay is one of the most lucid expositions on this complex subject.

Coleman, Elliott. *Lectures in Criticism.* New York: Harper Torchbooks/ The Bollingen Library, 1961. A symposium on criticism at Johns Hopkins University gave rise to this collection of essays. Herbert Read is responsible for the essay on Coleridge.

Cruse, Amy. *The Englishman and His Books in the Early Nineteenth Century.* New York: Crowell, n.d. For information concerning the facts of publication surrounding the emergence of significant books.

Daiches, David. *A Critical History of English Literature.* 2 vols. New York: The Ronald Press, 1960. Useful for a general overview of the Romantic movement, but note: no mention of Coleridge as dramatist.

Fogle, Richard Harter. *The Idea of Coleridge's Criticism.* Los Angeles: University of California Press, 1962. The most lucid study to date of Coleridge's criticism.

Gillman, James. *The Life of Samuel Taylor Coleridge.* London: William Pickering, 1838. The Gillman, who took Coleridge in during the last years of his life, writes without objectivity but relates anecdotes and incidents which could be known only to one who knew the poet well.

Gleckner, Robert F. and Gerald E. Enscoe. *Romanticism: Points of View.* Englewood Cliffs, New Jersey: Prentice-Hall, 1962. Essays on the topic by Pater, Babbitt, Grierson, Hulme, Lovejoy, Bernbaum, Fairchild, Lucas, Fogle, Wellek, Peckham, and others. Indispensable collection of many of the classic statements on Romanticism.

Griggs, Earl Leslie, ed., *Wordsworth and Coleridge: Studies in Honor of George McLean Harper.* Princeton: The University Press, 1939. Essays by distinguished Coleridge and Wordsworth scholars; some on peripheral aspects of the poets' lives.

Hanson, Lawrence. *The Life of S. T. Coleridge: the Early Years.* New

York: Oxford University Press, 1939. Most recent biography; covers only the early years.

James, D. G. *The Romantic Comedy*. New York: Oxford University Press, 1948. Part III on "The Gospel of Heaven" is one of the few, clear discussions of Coleridge's distinction between reason and understanding, pp. 155–270.

Jones, Edgar. "New Reading of 'Christabel,'" *Cambridge Journal*, V (November, 1951–1952), 97–112. Psychosexual interpretation of the poem.

Jordan, John E. *DeQuincey to Wordsworth: A Biography of a Relationship*. Berkeley: University of California Press, 1962. Interesting light on DeQuincey as critic of Coleridge and Wordsworth and as a rather unstable judge of the characters of men.

Lovejoy, Arthur O. *Essays in the History of Ideas*. New York: Capricorn Books, 1960. See especially "Coleridge and Kant's Two Worlds," pp. 254–76; also contains the essay, "On Discriminations of Romanticisms," pp. 228–53.

Lowes, John Livingston. *The Road to Xanadu*. New York: Vintage Books, 1959. First edition c. 1927 by Houghton Mifflin. This study of the sources of the "Ancient Mariner" and "Kubla Khan" has long been considered essential to any work done with these poems.

Marchand, Leslie A. *Byron*. 3 vols. New York: Alfred Knopf, 1957. Many anecdotes relating to the Lake Poets. In particular the anecdote of Shelley's reaction to the reading of "Christabel."

Mill, John Stuart. *On Bentham and Coleridge*, introduction by F. R. Leavis. New York: Harper Torchbooks, 1950. These essays are difficult to come by. This paperback collection makes them readily available to students. Fine early critical estimate of Coleridge is still valid for today.

Muirhead, John H. *Coleridge As Philosopher*. New York: Macmillan, 1930. Still the only full-length study of Coleridge as philosopher.

Nethercot, Arthur H. *The Road to Tryermaine*: a Study in the History, Background, and Purposes of Coleridge's "Christabel." Chicago: University of Chicago Press, 1939. Traditional reading of the poem as a work involved with the supernatural supernatural.

Nicoll, Allardyce. *A History of Early Nineteenth Century Drama: 1800–1850*. 2 vols. Cambridge, Mass.: Harvard University Press, 1930. Volume I treats of the history of the drama and includes useful appendices describing London and country theaters. Volume II lists places and dates of play productions.

————. *A History of Late Eighteenth Century Drama: 1750–1800*. Cambridge, Mass.: University Press, 1937. For Coleridge's early plays, production dates, number of editions, types, and so forth.

Praz, Mario. *The Romantic Agony*. Translated by Angus Davidson. London: Oxford University Press, 1933. A study of the frenetic and morbid aspect of Romanticism with particular attention to Satanic, sadistic elements and to the prevalence of the "fatal woman."

Radley, Virginia L. "*Christabel*: Directions Old and New," *Studies in English Literature*, (October, 1964), 531–41. Survey of past and present directions of *Christabel* scholarship with particular attention to the *Notebooks* as possible sources for support of one of the two alternate readings.

Raine, Kathleen. *Coleridge*. London: Longmans, Green, 1958. Clear biographical account.

Ransom, John Crowe. *The New Criticism*. Norfolk, Conn.: New Directions, 1941. Note discussion of "tension" differs from "tension" discussed in this study.

Renwick, W. L. *English Literature: 1789–1815*. Oxford: Clarendon, 1963. See for discussion of the poetry of Reverend Bowles.

Richards, Ivor A. *Coleridge On Imagination*. London: K. Paul, Trench, Trubner and Co., 1934. Actually this study is more Richards on Imagination than Coleridge. Ignores metaphysical aspects of the criticism.

Schneider, Elisabeth. *Coleridge, Opium, and "Kubla Khan."* Chicago: University Press, 1953. Opium and the extent to which it affected Coleridge's poetry. Delves into medical effects, history of opium, and so forth.

———. "The 'Dream' of 'Kubla Khan,'" *PMLA*, LX (September, 1945), 784–801. Early thoughts on effect of opium upon the poem.

Snyder, Alice D. *Coleridge On Logic and Learning*. New Haven: Yale University Press, 1929. Selections from unpublished manuscripts.

The Times Literary Supplement. Friday, July 26, 1963. Editorial commentary, "The Critical Moment," and subsequent articles by George Steiner, Rene Wellek, John Wain, Harry Levin, and L. C. Knights are valuable for gleaning some idea of the state of literary criticism today. Also serves to point out eminence of Coleridge as ancestor of much modern criticism.

Tuveson, Ernest Lee. *The Imagination as a Means of Grace*. Berkeley: University of California, 1960. On Locke and the esthetics of Romanticism.

Ward, A. W., ed., *Cambridge History of English Literature*. 15 vols. New York: G. P. Putnam's Sons, c. 1907–33. Vols. VIII (II) and Vol. XI used in this study.

Watson, E. Bradlee. *Sheridan to Robertson*. Cambridge: Harvard University Press, 1926. Excellent on causes for failure of the drama as art form in the nineteenth century. Stage history and related literary problems recounted.

Watson, George. *The Literary Critics.* London: Penguin, 1962. Essay on Wordsworth and Coleridge as literary critics is well worth reading. Discusses problems of working with critiques of Coleridge criticism.

Watson, Lucy Gillman. *Coleridge At Highgate.* New York: Longmans, Green, 1925. Some facts unavailable elsewhere given here by this relative of Dr. Gillman.

Whalley, George. "Coleridge Unlabyrinthed," *University of Toronto Quarterly,* XXXII (July, 1963), 325–45. Excellent summary bibliographic essay on Coleridge's publications. Incisive commentary on the "whole" Coleridge plus good bibliographic essay on the state of Coleridge scholarship today. Suggestions made for future scholarly endeavors.

Woodring, Carl R. *Politics in the Poetry of Coleridge.* Madison: University of Wisconsin Press, 1961.

Index

Aristotle, 32, 107

Baker, James V., 22, 109
Basler, Roy P., 67
Bate, Walter Jackson, 103, 106, 107
Bentham, Jeremy, 149–50
Berkeley, Bishop George, 23, 40
Blake, William, 13, 27, 29, 31
Bloom, Harold, 145
Boehme, Jacob, 23
Bowles, William, 14, 37
Boyer, J. B., 14
Brun, Fredericka, 86
Burke, Edmund, 37
Byron, George Gordon, Lord, 27, 93–94, 102–3

Cairn, Huntington, 107, 111
Campbell, James, 17, 20
Child, Harold, 93
Cleverness (Coleridgian category of men and nations), 140–41
Coburn, Kathleen, 77, 106, 149
Coleridge, Henry Nelson (nephew), 25, 136–37
Coleridge, Samuel Taylor, early life, 13–16; middle years, 16–24; later years, 24–26; religious development, 25; prose style, 105–6, 127, 142–43; illness, 17–26; criticism: miscellaneous English and world literature, 126–27; of Pope, 126; Shakespearean, 118–26; Wordsworthian, 114–18; philosophical influences on, 22–24, 40–41, 42–43, 128–42
WORKS OF:

Aids to Reflection, 25, 128–30, 134, 139
Anima Poetae, 137–38, 139
"Ballad of the Dark Ladie, The," 57, 80–83, 85
Biographia Literaria, 22–23, 25, 105, 108, 112, 128, 150
"Christabel," 19, 20, 24–25, 31, 57, 66–77, 145
Confessions of an Inquiring Spirit, 25
Conciones ad Populum, 16
Constitution of Church and State, 25
"Death of Wallenstein, The," 97, 146
"Dejection: An Ode," 20, 34, 87–92, 110, 144
"Destiny of Nations, The," 34, 39–40
"Effusion at Evening, An," 35
"Eolian Harp, The," 34, 44–47, 88, 91, 144
Fall of Robespierre, The, 16, 94–97
"Fears in Solitude," 34, 53–54, 145, 146
"France: An Ode," 34, 52–53
Friend, The, 21, 118, 139, 141–42
"Frost at Midnight," 34, 54–56, 144, 146
"Hints Toward the Formation of a More Comprehensive Theory of Life," 132
"Hymn Before Sunrise," 86
"Joan of Arc," 39
"Kubla Khan," 18–19, 24, 31, 57, 77–80, 145, 146

Index